# Truancy

Editor Barry Turner

Ward Lock Educational

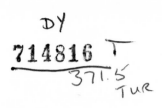

ISBN 0 7062 3404 9 casebound
0 7062 3405 7 paperback

First published 1974

Set in 11 on 12 point Journal Roman IBM
by Preface Limited, Salisbury
and Printed and bound in Great Britain
by Robert MacLehose & Co Ltd,
Anniesland, Glasgow
for Ward Lock Educational
116 Baker Street
London W1M 2BB
Made in England

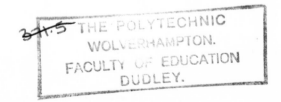

# Contents

*Barry Turner*

# Introduction

We used to talk about children *playing* truant, the impli-
cation being that kids were bound to get up to mischief and
that skipping classes once in a while — to watch a football
match or go to the cinema — was well within the category of
minor and easily forgiveable offences. The attendance officers,
who were supposed to take a hard line, were cast as mean
minded spoilsports — by children and even by parents and
teachers. But attitudes have changed. The voluntary absentee
can no longer rely on a large measure of good humoured
tolerance. Truancy has acquired the status of a social and
educational crisis. As Maurice Tyerman, our opening contri-
butor, points out in his survey of the predominant features of
the problem, ('Who are the truants?'), truancy is one of the
most popular subjects for television and newspaper investigation and in both England and Scotland major official
enquiries have been initiated.

This sudden rush of concern springs partly from a general
conviction that the numbers of children deliberately staying
away from school has increased substantially in recent years.
It is more a conviction than a fact because accurate
statistics are notoriously hard to come by, as Paul Williams
explains in his chapter 'Collecting the figures'. The traditional
school practice of ticking and crossing a list of names first
thing in the morning and afternoon tells us very little about
truancy as such. (Does Johnny really have a bad cold or is he
helping out at home?) And, anyway, many of the large urban
schools are unable to guarantee that even if Johnny is present
at 9.0 am he will still be on the premises after the first lesson.

Judging by teacher experience, it is a reasonable assumption that truancy is increasing, particularly in the cities. But
having said that, it is anyone's guess just how bad the
position is overall or in any particular area. Estimates vary

5

wildly and even within the confines of this text the closest we get to common agreement is that truancy is running at between 2 per cent and 5 per cent of all school children. In a new effort to provide a more informative statistical framework for discussion, Ken Richardson and Ken Fogelman of the National Children's Bureau have drawn up a comprehensive analysis which combines teacher assessment of truancy rates with an investigation into the link between school attendance and various aspects of school attainment. They find that absentees are more likely to come from families of the lower social groups, that truancy accounts for only a small proportion of all absences and that it affects boys more often than girls. Beyond these and other essential basic findings, the authors discover very low proportions of truants rated as above average or even average scholastic ability and, perhaps more significantly, that the proportion of truants from families where parents want their children to leave school is some six or seven times higher than the proportion of those whose parents want them to stay on.

Richardson and Fogelman are the first to admit that more, much more, research needs to be done before we can be satisfied that we are working with valid and reliable figures. Still, knowing that truancy is with us, to a greater or lesser extent, is a sufficient incentive to ask 'What should be done?' The answer from Dr Rhodes Boyson ('The need for realism') is to combine a strengthening of educational administration and discipline with the abolition of the law which requires children to stay on at school even when they are proved to be apathetic or hostile to further study. 'There is no reason,' says Rhodes Boyson, 'why at the age of fourteen, fifteen or sixteen a boy should not sit a school leaving certificate and, provided he has reached a minimum standard in English and mathematics and a reasonable standard of knowledge in all other subjects, has 95 per cent attendance for the previous three years and a job to go to, should not be allowed to leave immediately.'

The point is taken up by Frank Harris ('Rebels with a cause') who advocates work experience schemes which would allow youngsters to gain industrial experience while continuing their education on a part-time basis, with the possibility of returning to full-time education at a later age. Such schemes might enable all children, but in particular the reluctant learners, to recognize a link between the knowledge they acquire at school and its application in the world outside.

But neither Rhodes Boyson nor Frank Harris are arguing that the problem of truancy can be solved simply by pushing the reluctant learners in the direction of the factory gates. For one thing it is unreasonable to assume that the truant is merely antagonistic to the idea of learning. Sometimes there are other, more subtle causes which can and must be investigated as a matter of social urgency. In a set of four interviews ('Talking to truants') Jeremy Seabrook shows that the hard core truant can also be a damaged personality who cloaks his fear and despair with a show of blustering hostility. No one could reasonably assert that Trevor, the son of a work-shy drunk, who fought with his teachers ('it used to take three of them, just to hold me down') and stabbed a boy with a pen, would immediately be transformed into a new character if his truancy was somehow legalized and he was told to work at a conveyor belt instead of at a school desk.

Then again it is easy enough to assume that all the worst cases of absenteeism are extensions of antisocial behaviour, but there are otherwise apparently normal children who develop a fear of school that is so intense as to compel them to be persistent truants. The phenomenon is known as school phobia. It is described by Dr Jack Kahn ('School phobia or school refusal?') who says that the symptoms — the defeat by the child of all attempts to coerce attendance and the return to normal behaviour when absence from school is accepted — indicate intense conflict within the child-parent relationship. Unlike most truants who come from poorer homes and are of less than average intelligence, children with school phobia often have prosperous homes and are likely to be reasonably bright.

As in other cases of truancy, some form or other of remedial treatment can be provided for the sufferers of school phobia. But it is a major task locating and identifying the victims before their particular problems reach over-whelming proportions. The trouble is that so few professionals are involved in the business of helping children in trouble. As Frank Coombes points out ('Truancy on trial') a central figure in any concerted attack on the causes of truancy is the educational welfare officer. Yet for a total school population of over eight millions there are only 2,500 educational welfare officers. These are the people who used to be known as attendance officers and though their responsibilities have broadened over the years they still bear the image of law enforcing officers whose aim is to instill fear in delinquent children and delinquent parents. In fact, their greatest concern is for children who suffer parental neglect, which means that while truancy is still very much within the scope of their work, they are in a much stronger position to follow up investigations and make proposals for remedial action.

Following the recommendations of the Seebohm Report of 1968 there is now a general acknowledgment that schools need to be provided with a social work force capable of dealing with a wide range of family problems. But the cutback in the growth of education facilities makes this a remote prospect – at least, for the country as a whole. Meanwhile, the more adventurous and imaginative local education authorities are making a start by launching cooperative social worker/teacher enterprises which aim to breach the truancy statistics. Anna Sproule and Ruth Brandon ('Local authority experiments') describe projects in London and Liverpool that might well set the pattern for the development of remedial schemes in other LEAs.

Whatever success is achieved, there remains the nagging question of deciding just how much effort should be put into persuading the dropouts to conform to a system that they have already tried and rejected. Perhaps it is the system itself that needs adapting to take account of the special needs of the dissonant minority. In the concluding chapter Julia McGuinness makes a plea for the free schools as an alternative source of education for those who are disillusioned with conventional instruction. The informal and self-regulating environment associated with the free schools has been found to be particularly suitable for some problem children who might otherwise reject education altogether. And this, of course, begs the fundamental question for the state schools. If they are not equipped to help children in distress, should not they resolve to change their ways?

*Maurice Tyerman*

# Who are the truants?

In most countries of Europe the school leaving age is being raised to sixteen or over, and increasing numbers of pupils are voluntarily staying on beyond that age. School systems based on selection and segregation are losing favour against those which are said to be more democratic and egalitarian. And growing numbers of students are proceeding to further and higher education, though the rate of increase is slowing down. Yet at the same time as educational provision is extending and developing there is increasing debate about the whole philosophy of the educational system and increasing criticism of what is being offered in schools, colleges, polytechnics and universities. It is argued by some that standards of attainment are falling, and by others that education is so academic that it fails to meet the real needs of pupils and students. These needs, it is contended, are primarily emotional and social while schools reflect 'achievement-oriented attitudes' which should be rejected.

This debate is not confined to Britain; in fact it is probably less heated here than in many countries. The Carnegie Commission described schools in the United States as 'oppressive, grim and joyless' (Stevens 1972). There is a strong feeling that they do 'more harm than good' (Schwartz 1972). Education in the Netherlands and France has been criticized as being too competitive (Anon 1973a). And some writers argue that education as conceived at present is 'a myth to which the ritual of schooling corresponds' (Illich, quoted by Schwartz 1972, p. 167).

An added criticism heard of schools today is that at a time

when more is being spent on education than ever before, and when educational opportunities are greater than they have ever been, increasing numbers of children are truanting or their parents are keeping them at home, and that this is the school's fault. Despite obvious similarities, there are equally obvious differences between a child staying at home because her parents tell her to help in the house and a girl wandering into the streets and shops while allowing her parents to think she has gone to school. In the first case the offence is primarily the parents', in the second the child's. But truancy is frequently used to describe both these situations which accounts in part for the very different estimates that are made of its extent. In this discussion, truancy will be reserved to describe unjustified absence on a child's own initiative without the permission of parents or school.

There is also a distinction to be drawn between the child who truants on odd occasions for special reasons, and the child who persistently absents himself, even though here again one condition runs into the other. Truancy and parental withdrawal are also to be distinguished from school phobia, a neurotic fear of school that some writers believe has its origin in a child's ambivalent feelings towards his parents. It has been argued elsewhere (Tyerman 1968) that in many such cases fear arises from bullying or other un-pleasantness in school or on the way to school or home, rather than from neurotic conflict.

Poor attendance makes for poor progress and for difficulty in forming friendly links with other children. The typical persistent truant is unhappy at home, unpopular at school, and unsuccessful in his classwork. He is rarely an articulate critic of contemporary society and its educational values. He is usually a child failing to cope satisfactorily with his difficulties and in need of help. A similar view comes from Sweden (Marklund 1973):

> The pupil who plays truant is generally a difficult, anxious and highly sensitive person who needs to escape from reality. He also has a low status in class and has difficulties in his dealing with other people there.

He wanders away from these difficulties and in at least half the cases drifts into delinquency (e.g. Monroe 1973). Truancy is the 'kindergarten of crime' (Healy 1915). Irregular

10

school attendance for whatever cause is a distress call (Tyerman 1968).

All countries contain a number of parents and children who regard going to school as a burden to be endured rather than an opportunity to be grasped. They are recognized as constituting a problem about which more should be known. Yet there has been little research into absence or truancy either in this country or the rest of Europe, in Canada or the United States. It has usually been studied as an aspect of a wider problem such as educational retardation, deprivation, adolescent behaviour, or delinquency. The much less common problem of school phobia has received far greater academic interest. It is typical that Blanco (1972) devotes seven pages to school phobia but only one and a half to truancy in his prescriptions for children with learning and behaviour problems. In the last two years in the UK there have been only two published accounts of research into the topic (Davie 1972 and Mitchell 1972), though there have been several discussion papers. As a result there is a plethora of opinions and almost a dearth of facts.

With the raising of the school leaving age, truancy in Britain, particularly by fifteen year olds, has become news. It has been the subject of two television programmes, and a feature on a number of others; there seems to be some reference to it in the newspapers nearly every day. In Scotland it is to be the subject of a public enquiry. In England the Department of Education and Science has, as a special measure, asked all maintained secondary schools to state for a particular day in January 1974 the numbers of possible attendances and the numbers that were actually made, by boys and girls separately, and for each age group. Schools were also asked to indicate the number of absences for which they knew of no legitimate reason. The results will become available towards the end of 1974.

Enquiries into the extent of absence have also recently been made by a number of local authorities and professional organizations, but the results are unpublished. Reports that are available indicate that throughout the country the overall annual percentage of attendance is about 91, and that there is no sign of a general decline in attendance though, of course, this may be occurring in certain schools and certain areas. In primary schools attendance is about 0.5 per cent higher than

11

the overall average and about the same percentage lower for secondary schools. Attendance in the autumn term tends to be a little higher than in the summer term and in both terms it is higher than in spring. Grammar schools tend to have better attendance figures than comprehensive schools, and their attendance seems better than that of secondary modern schools. Attendance decreases as pupils become older, especially if they are in the lower sets or streams. Truancy appears to be responsible for about 2 per cent of absences overall and for much more than this in certain forms of certain schools in certain areas.

The ILEA appears to have special difficulties and to have received most press coverage. The chairman of an ILEA subcommittee has stted that two out of five children play truant in some London schools during their last year, but he emphasized that in other schools the absentee rate was not 'markedly out of line' with the average attendance level within the authority of 88–90 per cent (*Daily Telegraph* April 2, 1974). A recent survey of 165 secondary schools throughout the country by the Headmasters Association also found wide variation between schools in their truancy rates, from a rural grammar school with less than 1 per cent of children who sometimes truanted to a city centre comprehensive with 12 per cent. The survey concluded that 'when all factors have been considered, the fact remains that the larger a school the greater the proportion of pupils with low attendance records'.

It may be that with the raising of the leaving age there are among persistent truants, as distinct from children whose parents allow them to stay away from school, considerable numbers of mature, competent young people who have outgrown school, but there is no hard, published eviden ce to prove the point. Equally, while teachers find certain pupils difficult and are not sorry when they are absent there are no firm grounds for the rumour that many schools can only keep going because many fifteen and sixteen year old pupils are absent, many after attending for registration, and that if these pupils did return the teachers could not cope with them.

The North West Regional Society of Education Officers (1971) reported that the overall percentage of attendance in their area in May 1971 was 92.9. Truancy was estimated to account for approximately 5 per cent of absence and parents keeping their children from school without good reason for 15 per cent. Eighteen per cent of all pupils were absent some time during the week; 26 per cent from special schools, 25 per cent from modern schools, 24 per cent from comprehensive schools, 16 per cent from primary schools, and 15 per cent from selective secondary schools. Three per cent were absent once, 7 per cent twice, 1 per cent three times, 7 per cent four times, 1 per cent six times and 3 per cent ten times. A similar overall figure to that from England was reported by Mitchell (1972) from her study of seven secondary schools in central Scotland. Only one of the schools had an absence rate greater than 10 per cent. Nearly a fifth of the absentees were away from school to help at home or for other unsatisfactory reasons.

Mitchell (1972), like other investigators, found that poor attenders are most likely to come from large families where the father is a manual worker, and that absence increases as a child approaches school leaving age. Davie et al (1972) also reported differences in attendance rates between social classes. In their sample of seven year old children in the National Child Development Study, 75 per cent of the pupils in social class I made 91 per cent attendance or above, 67 per cent in class II, 70 per cent in class III (nonmanual), 62 per cent in class IV and 61 per cent in class V. There was little difference between the attendance of boys compared with that of girls. The same pattern was seen when these children were eleven years of age: 87 per cent of the middle-class pupils made 90 per cent attendance or better, 79 per cent of the children of skilled or semiskilled manual workers and 71 per cent of the children of unskilled manual workers. Attendance habits seem to persist. Only 13 per cent of good attenders at seven were poor attenders at eleven. Davie (1972) also reported differences between regions of the country with 51 per cent of seven year old pupils in Scotland making 96—100 per cent attendance compared with 35 per cent in Wales. Averages can mislead. An attendance figure of 88 per cent meant in one school that 54 per cent of pupils were absent at least once in the week (anon 1973).

The causes of truancy are to be found in the home, in the school, and in the child's personality. His relations with his parents and their attitudes are of particular importance. Each *leadership* case has its own special features though certain characteristics are usually found. Every truant should be considered as an individual and given the help that his own particular circumstances demand. Over the past few years this principle seems to have had growing acceptance and is reflected in the number of different approaches to help truants. One obvious measure is court proceedings. These are very rarely taken, and then usually only in the most extreme cases with varying effect.

Another obvious approach is to lower the school leaving age. This is advocated by some social workers and professional organizations. Others contend that fifteen year old pupils should be allowed to leave if their future employers would ensure that they attend a college of education on day release. It has also been argued that the school-leaving age should be made more flexible, and that when pupils have taken their GCE or CSE examinations in June they should be allowed to leave. The use of tribunals as in New Zealand or special permission for selected cases as in Sweden has been suggested.

*why?* It is a matter for debate whether the advantage to those children who might be helped by being allowed to leave school would be balanced by the opportunities denied to others because of pressure from their parents to leave school and take a job. Most persistent truants are not precocious youths, but maladjusted children who would become unsatisfactory employees instead of being unsatisfactory pupils. The psychiatric and psychological services do not have the staff to help all these maladjusted truants and the many hundreds of thousands of other children with personal difficulties. There are less than 650 educational psychologists and 200 child psychiatrists in the country. To make the best use of these slender resources the traditional organization and practice of child guidance is changing and a network of interrelated services is now envisaged with the psychologist spending less time in clinics and centres and more in schools and other places where children gather together, helping children directly and also giving indirect help through advice to teachers and parents. The emphasis will increasingly be on prevention (DES 1971). But these future plans are of limited value to the child who is truanting now and the child guidance services will never be able to help all the children who are in need.

Increasingly in the past two years the thought has developed that if a child cannot cope in the traditional school let him be offered an alternative form of education, either to prepare him for his return to the ordinary school or as a complete substitute for it. In the first category are sanctuaries in primary and secondary schools, attended by selected children for all or part of the day, intermediate treatment or education centres for truants referred to them, educational guidance centres for disruptive children, transitional classes attached to child guidance centres, nurture groups, and day-care centres. Some of these are becoming integral parts of their education authority's provision. In the second category are some free schools, so-called because the children are free to decide whether to join or not, free to decide when to come, free to decide how the school should be run and free to learn what they want to learn. Such schools are financed in part by voluntary subscription, and indirectly by various social agencies. Many of the teachers give their services free. Mention must also be made of family advice centres staffed by detached social workers operating within the community with local authority support. Their purposes seem particularly directed towards estranged youth and their families. In some cases, these social workers deal with children during school hours in an informal group.

These centres, classes and schools seem to be directed particularly towards children who are seriously disturbed, and they have certain features in common, though of course they differ in emphasis from one group to another. Perhaps most important are an acceptance of the child and his difficulties, organization in small groups, and a warm, informal relationship between pupil and teacher. There is insufficient evidence to show how well they are succeeding in diagnosing and treating a child's educational difficulties, integrating into the work of the class the assistance of the whole range of welfare services that are available to a family and child, and how far they have been able to help their pupils' personal development. They are too few and too untried to be available for more than a few truants. It is clear that the main source of help for truants must be the ordinary school itself working closely with the education welfare officer, the social, psychological and medical services, both statutory and voluntary, and attempting to enlist the aid of the parents.

Within schools there must be careful registration, possibly more than once during each morning or afternoon, and speedy notification of absentees to an education welfare officer to enable the cause of an unexplained absence to be quickly investigated. They are key figures. There is also the need to reexamine in some schools certain parts of the curriculum, and the general teaching-learning approach so that all pupils can achieve some measure of success, and thus self-respect, in something they feel is worthwhile. In each school, particularly where there are pupils of secondary age, an effective system of pastoral care should be organized. In primary schools this usually develops without a formal structure through the children spending much of their time with one teacher. In secondary schools it needs to be deliberately established, preferably with a trained counsellor at its centre, and based on teachers who are given time for their pastoral duties and training as for any other aspect of their work.

In trying to understand the feelings and difficulties of their adolescent pupils teachers face particular difficulties. Young people are suspicious of adult pretensions; they challenge and question. Many face difficulty arising from physical maturity coupled with emotional immaturity and conflicts then arise with home, school and the law. The form their behaviour takes will often be determined by the current fashions and values within the age group. An added difficulty in dealing with adolescents is that an adult is confronted with aspects of his own growing up that he has not resolved. Teachers are willing to help children who approach them. They must be enabled, through in-service courses and through regular discussions in the school with members of the support services in the area, to recognize a child in distress, to go to him and know how to help him.

This short survey has outlined some features of truancy in the light of current developments in education, and offered some possible answers to this perennial problem. Many aspects that have only been touched upon here have been covered more deeply in the publications listed in the bibliography. Two truths are inescapable. First, to problems in education there are rarely quick and easy solutions; only different approaches. Second, prevention is better than cure. In the case of truancy and many other disorders of childhood and adolescence, the key to this prevention lies in the child

16

knowing that he belongs in his home and school, that he
counts for something, and that his parents and his teachers
care about him and are trying to do their best for him. In the
home parental love and standards that are worth following,
and in the school a sense of purpose and concern for the
individual child, are powerful influences for good.


*References*

ANON (1973) Truancy: what the official figures don't show
   *Where?* 82, 228–9
ANON (1973a) Symposium highlights dropout issues
   (Account of proceedings of Council of Europe's Sympo-
   sium on the Education of the 16–19 age group) *Times
   Educational Supplement* 3045, 17
BANKS, C. and FINLAYSON, D. (1973) *Success and Failure
   in the Secondary School* London: Methuen
BLANCO, R. F. (1972) *Prescription for Children with
   Learning and Adjustment Problems* Springfield, Illinois:
   Thomas
DAVIE, R., BUTLER, N. and GOLDSTEIN, H. (1972) *From
   Birth to Seven* London: Longman
DAVIE, R. (1972) Absence from school *Education Guardian*
   September 12
DES (1974) *Child Guidance* (Circular 3/74) London: HMSO
GUNSELL, R. *et al* (1973) *Intermediate Treatment Centre:
   Second Report 1972–3* Unpublished
HEALY, W. (1915) *The Individual Delinquent* London:
   Heinemann
HOLDEN, H. M. (1972) A note on alientated youth *Journal
   of Child Psychology and Psychiatry* 13, 289, 297
JACQUES, A. (1971) 'Attendance' in *The Enclyclopedia of
   Education Volume 1* New York: Macmillan and Free Press
JENCKS, C. *et al* (1973) *Inequality* London: Allen Lane
KAUFMAN, Laura (1973) Action team on call for behaviour
   problems *Education* 141, 520
LAW, W. B. (1973) An alternative to truancy *British Journal
   of Guidance and Counselling* 1, 91–6
LYONS, K. H. (1973) *Social Work and the School* London:
   HMSO
MACBEATH, J. (1973) Free schools for accountability
   *Times Educational Supplement* 3030, 4

MARKLUND, S. (1972) *School Fatigued Pupils* Unpublished

MEDLICOTT, P. (1973) The truancy problem *New Society* 25, 768—70

MITCHELL, S. (1972) The absentees *Education in the North* 9, 22—8

MONROE, J. E. (1973) 'A study of the relationship between truancy and delinquency with reference to a particular comprehensive school for boys since the coming into force of the main sections of the 1969 Children and Young Persons Act' Unpublished thesis for the Diploma in Criminology, University of London

MORTON-WILLIAMS, R. *et al* (1968) *Young School Leavers* London: HMSO

NORTH WEST REGIONAL SOCIETY OF EDUCATION OFFICERS (1971) Investigation into the incidence of irregular school attendance in the north-west area during the week ending May 7, 1971 (Unpublished)

RALPHSON, H. (1973) School absenteeism in a remedial department *Remedial Education*, 8, 29

REIMER, E. (1971) *School is Dead* Harmondsworth: Penguin

RICHMOND, W. K. (1973) *The Free School* London: Methuen

SCHWARTZ, B. N. (1972) 'Deschooling: a conversation with Ivan Illich' in B. Schwartz (Ed) *Affirmative Education* New Jersey: Prentice Hall

SCOTT, G. (1974) Truant centres cost a lot but they are worth it *Times Educational Supplement* 3064, 14

STEVENS, W. K. (1972) 'Review of the Carnegie Commission Report' in B. Schwartz (Ed) *Affirmative Education* New Jersey: Prentice Hall

TYERMAN, M. J. (1968) *Truancy* London: University of London Press

TYERMAN, M. J. (1972) Absent from school *Trends in Education* 26, 14—20

VAUGHAN, M. and HILL, F. (1973) Forward from the Summerhill experiment *Times Educational Supplement* 3015, 10

VAUGHAN, M. (1974) ILEA help for truancy centres *Times Educational Supplement* 3059,6

WALL, W. D. *et al* (1973) The problem child and the psychological services *Educational Review* 2, 1—60

WEDGE, P. and PROSSER, H. (1973) *Born to Fail* London: Arrow

WEST, D. J. and FARRINGTON, D. P. (1973) *Who Becomes Delinquent?* London: Heinemann

WISEMAN, D. (1969) *The Welfare of the School Child* Unpublished (obtainable from Institute of Education, Exeter)

*Paul Williams*

# Collecting the figures

The girl on the bus was telling her friends how she had been caught sneaking out of school after registration.

'The deputy found me just as I was going out of the gates,' she said. 'She sent me straight to the head.'

'What happened then?' asked a friend.

'She asked me why I was leaving school, and I told her my cat was sick. She told me to go home and look after it.'

Collapse of schoolgirls in laughter.

In that story, told to me by a juvenile magistrate who also happened to be on the bus, one can find the essence of the problem of collecting figures about truancy.That girl had been playing truant. But where would she show on the statistics? Not on the register, where she was marked as present. Her absence from classes was not recorded. And what if it had been noted? It would be put down as justified, though of course it was not. So she escapes being put down as a truant. And throughout the country there are thousands of boys and girls in the same situation. But if truancy figures are to mean much, that girl must appear somewhere and in the right category.

The first problem that greets anyone wanting to study the extent of truancy in schools is the disagreement between experts on what truancy really is. The word implies a degree of malice so, some would argue, a school phobic is not a truant. He cannot help hating school, he has a physical revulsion to it. He is not malicious. On the other hand, school days are not always the happiest of one's life. So who is to

20

say when a simple dislike of school becomes a phobia? The argument continues as different people find different reasons for excluding children from being classed as truants.

Some would define truancy as avoidance of school without the knowledge of parents, but equally important in any study is avoidance *with* the knowledge of parents, and even avoidance *inspired* by parents. To get over this problem of definition, educationists use terms such as 'unjustified' or 'unacceptable' absence, but without saying what is justified or acceptable. When I asked one organization if they had carried out any research into the incidence of truancy, I was told no, but they had been looking into absenteeism! For the purposes of this chapter I shall use the word truancy to cover the whole problem, without entering into the discussion of who is and who is not a truant.

In the early days of education the most worrying aspect of truancy was that it reduced the grant paid to a school. The grant depended on results and attendance, and the importance of registers was simply that the ticks were translated into hard cash. There was an economic spur to get the children into the schools, for the greater the success of the school attendance officers, (or board men as they were called) in persuading recalcitrant pupils to attend school, the greater the grant. The attendance figures would go to the school board, which would discuss them with money uppermost in their minds. They would be as concerned about an outbreak of measles as of truancy.

The issue of truancy then seemed much simpler. It was met with liberal use of the cane. If the children thought there were more interesting things to do than go to those new fangled schools, they would have to learn the painful way that it did not matter, school was good for them. In those days many a head would observe in his log book that the advent of a fair nearby resulted in high truancy figures. Without any training in statistics he would make the obvious and correct conclusion: children preferred a fair to school.

Today our needs are much more sophisticated. Truancy is seen as a serious sociological problem, which can lead to juvenile delinquency and ultimately to crime. The causes are thought to be far more complex: living conditions, class distinctions, even the role of the school, are all questioned.

There is a growing desire to get to grips with the very roots of the problem.

The desire is growing, but it is not universal. There are still many local education authorities and headteachers who are reluctant to talk about truancy, and who do not want to know what the figures really are. They are protected in their complacency by the inaccuracy of the system of monitoring truancy that is used in every school — the register.

The payment by results system has died, but the register survives. It is at best only a rough guide; it has some serious deficiencies. Thus the figures are not really good enough for researchers, or for the local authorities who want to do something more constructive about truancy.

The most serious deficiency of the register is that it misses completely the children who skip class after the count is taken at the beginning of the morning and afternoon sessions. There is little doubt that this is a sizeable problem, particularly in the areas which suffer most from truancy. In fact, speaking purely from a statistical point of view, one can distinguish two types of absentee: the one who is absent at registration, and the one who goes to school to register and leaves afterwards. The absentees with genuine excuses (illness mainly), the parental-inspired truant, the most disturbed cases such as the school phobics, will all fall in the first category. In the second category will be the children who plan their truanting in an effort not to be caught out, clearly just as important a part of the problem.

In one school I know the head became so fed up with the postregistration exodus that one day he mounted a special exercise. The escape routes were all well known, and he with other teachers hid in ambush, catching the children as they left. It is significant that this was just a one off, special exercise. At other times the exodus went on uninterrupted, and the truants were left to their own devices.

A leaflet prepared for an antitruancy campaign in the Tower Hamlets division of the Inner London Education Authority illustrates this vividly, with a picture of children dropping out of a school window. The campaign came after an ILEA survey (October 1971) which specifically tackled the problem of postregistration truancy. Schools were asked, among other things, to note the number of children who had been marked as present and were missing at later lessons.

Out of 151,953 children an average of 315 skipped class after registration. It was enough for the report on the survey to say the numbers of postregistration truants were a cause for concern in some schools, and that there should be better control in those schools. It also concluded that it would be dangerous to extrapolate by applying figures from a limited survey to all schools. It found there was no close relationship between postregistration truancy and overall absenteeism, no significant correlation with levels of ability and attainment, and that no type of school was immune from this kind of truancy. Teachers in schools which have a truancy problem and who feel that not enough is being done say that the authorities are being lulled into a false sense of security by relying on attendance registers.

The second failure of registers is that in most cases there is no indication of the reasons for absence, even if they are known. Often there is not even the roughest indication as to whether an excuse has been proferred, whether a child is genuinely ill, whether the parents or the child is at fault, or whether the school has taken any action.

Without an elementary breakdown of reasons, it is dangerous to draw conclusions for individual schools. A school can have an outbreak of nits; flu might be sweeping the district; there might be a dispute between the LEA and parents (in two surveys I noted warnings that the figures are distorted by a 'strike' with parents refusing to send children to school in protest at transport arrangements). Parents differ over how long a child should be kept at home with a minor illness. It has been suggested that a middle class mother is less likely to keep a child away with a cold than a working class mother. So a school in a working class area would tend to have a lower attendance record than a school in a middle class area. The figures can be easily misinterpreted.

Absences are given in terms of 'pupil sessions' with two sessions a day. Six absences could be one pupil away for three days or six pupils taking the afternoon off to go to the races or to serve in the local market. This is the third failure. A simple check of the number of absences does not show how many children are involved. It could be a few pupils for much of the time, or many pupils spasmodically avoiding school.

The point was reinforced in an article in *Where?* by a local authority officer. He said that a school might have a 90 per cent attendance record, but over half its children truanting. He added that the occasional absences are more likely to be truancy.

The same point was made earlier in the ILEA survey which stated:

It is fair to say that not enough attention has been given to the occasional absence of children for no good reason. There is perhaps an attitude both on the part of parents, schools and society generally that such absences do not matter too much. This is by no means peculiar to London.

Despite all these reservations, the attendance register is still the start for most research. It has to be, because there are no other figures kept as a matter of routine that could be consulted to throw light on truancy. For example, the case loads of educational welfare officers can only be a guide to the number of hard core cases referred to them, and the number of prosecutions are only the tip of a large iceberg. So, if the LEA does want to monitor the situation, it turns to the attendance figures which can at least give an indication of something wrong. If attendance falls dramatically, the school needs some sort of extra help, even if it is extra visits from school nursing staff to fight nits.

What would be needed for really accurate figures? A register in every class, an investigation of every absence, and someone to put the figures together. It would take some more of everyone's time, and a lot of a few people's time. With a teacher shortage in the educationally deprived areas, and pressure to increase rather than decrease the proportion of a teacher's time spent teaching, such a regular and detailed system is ruled out as impracticable. But it should prove possible, when counting the number of absences, to count at the same time the number of children who have missed a session. And it should be feasible to give more indication of the reasons, even if it is not a complete rundown of causes of absence.

The other way of meeting the problem is to carry out the occasional study, and extrapolate from there. A number of such studies have been carried out, by researchers, LEAs and teachers' organizations. But generalizations are dangerous. The factors affecting truancy are so varied that some statistical sins may be committed when results of a limited survey are applied universally.

Surveys that do try to isolate causes rely on two main methods: a group of truants already receiving attention is given an even closer look or heads are asked to classify absences by causes.

In 1971–2 the Kingston upon Hull Headteachers Association carried out a survey of the second type, following discussion about the standards of behaviour in schools. It covered a term and a half. The questionnaire sought the numbers of children absent at home for 90 per cent of the time, 30 per cent or more and less than 30 per cent but with occasional absences over ten weeks. It asked whether the children were truanting with or without the knowledge of their parents, whether the absences were avoidable or unavoidable, and how they correlated with the parent preparing the child for school, or the child preparing himself. There was also a detailed analysis of reasons for absences in junior high schools.

The survey, which revealed a 13.6 per cent absentee rate for children aged thirteen to sixteen and a 3.3 per cent rate for those in the five to eight group, concluded that well over half the absences were avoidable. In many instances the heads did not know reasons why children stayed away. Also there was some confusion in the categories they customarily used, which is hardly surprising in view of the difficulties of defining the different types of absentee.

Also in 1971 the ILEA carried out their survey, mentioned above, which investigated absences on one day, October 15. One question asked was whether the absences were for illness, other acceptable reasons, or unacceptable and unknown reasons. But the answers were not very helpful. The report concluded:

> Unfortunately the nature of many of the school returns makes it impossible to separate the unacceptable and the unknown. It is likely that a number of children absent for unknown reasons would have acceptable reasons.

In fact following up some absences it was discovered that a few children had moved out of the area and on to new schools, but had not removed from their old school roll.

There are some national surveys in progress which may throw some light on the problem over the whole country, but even these have not really surmounted the obstacle of defining accurately what they want to know. Following the Children and Young Persons Act of 1969, the Association of Education Committees is surveying the problems of LEAs in enforcing school attendance. Replies on the incidence of absence and avoidance are being processed by the Department of Education and Science. Then there is the DES's own survey, a couple of questions tacked on to the annual Form Seven for 1974. The Department asks for the numbers of all absentees and unjustified absentees on January 17. Unjustified absentees it defines as 'absentees for whose absence the school knew of no legitimate reason by Wednesday January 23 . . .' and includes those who have not returned to school by January 23 with an excuse.

But almost certainly many schools will have simply taken the figures from the register, and ignored the postregistration truants. And what is a legitimate reason, anyway? It all depends on the attitude of the head and parents. Is school phobia a legitimate reason? Fear of bullying? Inability to face a particular teacher? A sick cat? Presumably a child who is classified as a school phobic, and is under the care of the psychologist or psychiatrist, and misses school, is away for a legitimate reason. But what if he is on the waiting list for the specialists? And what of the children for whom the parents provide excuses? Those who are told to stay at home to look after a sick parent or help around the house? What if the head does not believe the sick note? And is it legitimate for the mother to take her child away for the afternoon because she wants to go into town to buy some shoes?

In any survey into absenteeism the reasons are vitally important. But to find these reasons each individual absentee needs to be investigated — a huge task. So the question of deciding what is justified is left to the individual heads. Much will depend on their individual views and the extent to which they are in touch with individual children.

One survey by a local education authority carried out this

year (1974) does not ask for figures at all. It asks what heads think is going on, rather than what is actually going on. It asks whether the heads think truancy exists, whether they differentiate between types of truancy and to what extent parents approve the truancy. It will not find out the statistics of truancy in the LEA, but it should discover something about attitudes, and here it touches on an important point.

Truancy is a very complex problem. In order to carry out valid surveys and coming to conclusions from those surveys, it is necessary to understand what is going on in the individual school. In the primary schools, classes stay together after registration. There is less opportunity for skipping classes, and more likelihood of the teacher noticing absentees. But in secondary schools the pupils may be set. They move to specialist classrooms and change teachers and classes. A teacher of, say, a midmorning lesson may assume that if any chasing up has to be done, it is already in hand. The fact that Jones is leaving school after registration may only be discovered in a chance conversation in the staffroom. The experienced truant will know which teachers check up, and which do not, and will organize his truanting to evade detection.

Jones may also be the most disruptive child in the class. He may, to quote an education officer writing in *Where?* 'fill a lesson full of lead at fifty paces'. Far from being concerned, the teacher is happy that he is away, and does not wish to alter the situation. The head himself may be overburdened with the size and problems of his school. He may be one of the few who is simply unable to cope, or one of the many who feel that present thinking on corporal or other punishment makes it impossible for him to cope. If he knows the most disruptive children are out of school, he too may turn a blind eye. In the words of one deputy head, 'If we know they are truanting, we do not lean on them too hard.'

If a school is on a split site, with children having to walk from one building to the other, there is even more opportunity for truanting. And then there are unsupervised study periods. The ILEA survey commented that one grammar school head had revised his private study arrangements as a result of the survey.

But what of the educational welfare officers, successors to the school attendance officers, and sometimes still known as the 'board men'? In one LEA they were reorganized, and decided to leave it to the schools to refer cases to them. The result was they had so little work, they had to revert to going into the schools and studying the books. But if an EWO has enough work, he is less likely to search for more in the registers. And with the new law on taking children to court (the Children and Young Persons Act 1969) there are reports that they are finding their job far more difficult.

So in a deprived area you have teachers who are not looking for trouble, heads who have too much to do, EWOS who already have their hands full and cannot take more work. You also have more truants, with more of them going undetected and only the hard core receiving attention. In effect all the problems that make the collection of truancy figures so unreliable are magnified in those schools with the most truancy.

And here is one last thought on truancy figures: recent developments leading to schools going part-time, because of teachers' refusal to cover vacancies, have created a completely new type of truant — the child who truants from home. He is the boy or girl who is sent away from school, probably with some work to do, but omits to tell his parents he will be coming home. One head, asked about this in a television programme, told the interviewer, 'We have no guarantee that parents know. . . .'

*Ken Fogelman and Ken Richardson*

# School attendance: some results from the National Child Development Study

When in 1870 W. E. Forster addressed the House of Commons during his introduction to the Elementary Education Bill, he referred to the 'startling principle' of compulsory attendance. The proposed School Boards were for the first time to have powers of framing bye-laws for the compulsory attendance in school of children between the ages of five and thirteen. They were also given powers for fixing the school-leaving age, and for recruiting the forerunners of our modern education welfare officers (Curtis 1967, Maclure 1967). In fact, a substantial proportion of the School Boards failed to avail themselves of these powers until Lord Sandon's Act of 1876, but many others made strident efforts to boost attendance rates. The Board in Leeds, for example, was soon able to increase attendance rates from 64 per cent to 89 per cent amongst children on the school roll (Curtis 1966); such rates became a measure of success of School Boards and throughout the country attendance rates have been followed keenly ever since.

At least four major Acts and several amendments have since made special reference to school attendance. The Butler Education Act of 1944 stated explicitly that, 'It shall be the duty of the parent of every child of compulsory school age to cause him to receive efficient full-time education suitable to his age, ability and aptitude either by regular attendance at school or otherwise.' In fact a careful analysis of the Act reveals the difficulty of defining what 'full-time education' actually means, and ambiguities of interpretation have produced several High Court actions (Taylor and Saunders

1965, West 1966, Baker 1964). In spite of the increasing comprehensiveness of legislation, however, attendance rates have remained remarkably constant at around the 90 per cent level, and local authorities have found it difficult to improve them. On the other hand, many writers have emphasized the difficulty of obtaining fully representative national statistics on attendance rates and such studies as have been completed have tended to be restricted to localized regions or special groups of children (Clyne 1970, Tyerman 1968). The aim of this chapter, therefore, is to provide a broad statistical framework of attendance rates, together with some estimates of truancy and related features of school attainment, for a nationally representative sample of school children.

*The National Child Development Study*
Our information on school attendance is drawn from the longitudinal study known as the National Child Development Study, carried out by the National Children's Bureau. The study sample is composed of 16,000 children (over 98 per cent of contemporary births in the United Kingdom) born in one week of March 1958. These children and their sociomedical circumstances were studied intensively at that time in a survey of perinatal problems, funded by the National Birthday Trust (Butler and Bonham 1963, Butler and Alberman 1969). A followup study of the childrens' physical, social and educational development was carried out when the children were seven years old (Davie, Butler and Goldstein 1972); a second followup was completed four years later and a third is now in progress. The information presented here was collected during the second followup when the children were eleven years old and in the final year of primary schooling.

Our data have three components. The first consists of overall attendances compiled by teachers from school registers in the contemporary school year (1968—9). The second is drawn from statements of teachers as to whether or not the study child in question is known to have truanted or is suspected of truancy. These are related to, for example, the background and characteristics of the children and indices of parental interest. Finally we present the results of an analysis of the association between attendance rates and aspects of school attainment as assessed by standardized attainment tests. These last analyses represent a preliminary report only; the information is being subjected to a more detailed scrutiny by members of the NCDS research team at the present time.

*Attendance rates*

At the time of the second followup teachers were asked to report the number of possible attendances for each study child pertaining to that school year, and also the number of absences recorded. From these returns we have computed attendance rates for each child. Many of the returns had to be excluded from the final analysis, however, because of various anomalies and unreliabilities, but we have confirmed that the residual group of nearly 9,000 children is fully representative of the cohort with respect to such variables as region, social class, sex and type of school attended.

*Table 1  Distribution within social classes (percentaged)*

| Attendance rate % | I | II | III NM | III M | IV | V |
|---|---|---|---|---|---|---|
| Less than 85 | 6.3 | 5.7 | 5.1 | 10.3 | 11.5 | 19.8 |
| 85–95 | 27.4 | 33.7 | 33.3 | 36.3 | 37.9 | 34.7 |
| Greater than 95 | 66.2 | 60.6 | 61.6 | 53.5 | 50.6 | 45.6 |
| | 100.0 | 100.0 | 100.0 | 100.0 | 100.0 | 100.0 |
| N = | 386 | 1330 | 717 | 3383 | 1349 | 481 |

Social class is defined according to the Registrar General's Classification

I Professional groups
II Intermediate and management groups
III NM  skilled nonmanual
III M  skilled manual
IV semiskilled (manual)
V unskilled manual

Table 1 shows the distribution of attendance rates for each social class (the latter are defined according to the Registrar General's classification). These results reflect the expected distributions, with the proportion of poor attenders (defined as less than 85 per cent possible attendance) being some two to three times higher among those children whose fathers had manual occupations compared with nonmanual groups.

Similarly, a much greater proportion of the nonmanual groups was found to have attendance rates higher than 95 per cent. This social class distribution agrees with the reports of several other writers; Tyerman (1968) found that absence on the whole was twice as high among children of unskilled fathers compared with those of professional fathers, and parallels are found in the National Survey of Health and Development (Douglas 1964, Douglas and Rose 1966) and in a variety of *ad hoc* surveys summarized by Clyne (1968). The attendance rates as a whole correspond with those of Plowden (1966) which reported that 70 per cent of primary school children in their survey had over 90 per cent attendance, 9 per cent having less than 80 per cent attendance.

Table 2a (page 33) presents the distribution of attendance rates in each regional area. These data indicate that the attendance of children in the sample was highest in the south and south-west of England (with the north Midlands next in the list), and lowest in Wales and the north-west of England.

Comparison with other research in the regional context is difficult because of lack of correspondence in circumscribed districts of survey. In the National Survey, however, Douglas and Ross (1968) have similarly reported the lowest attendance rates in Wales, though they also report low attendance in the Midlands and south which is somewhat at variance with the present data. No doubt gross regional figures conceal many subregional extremes (Tennent 1972, Tyerman, 1968). Rankin (1961), for example, found attendance rates in county boroughs to be less than those in counties. They will certainly conceal the well-documented variations within authorities between schools (Plowden 1966), between classes in the same school (Tyerman 1972) and between the occupational groups which predominate in small circumscribed areas (Clyne 1968). The data presented, therefore, project a regional breakdown of the national returns, but those for each region represent the summation of a spectrum of largely unknown factors. As a result, it is precarious to speculate why, for example, Wales should have the lowest attendance rate. Is it the social class composition? Or perhaps the ratio of rural to urban population? Only further analysis will answer this question. It is known, however, that Welsh schools have a favourite teacher/pupil ratio, compared with the rest of Britain, owner occupation in Wales is higher than

*Table 2a  Distribution of attendance within regions (percentaged)*

| Attendance rate % | Region | | | | | | | | | | |
|---|---|---|---|---|---|---|---|---|---|---|---|
| | NW | N | EWR | NM | E | LSE | S | SW | M | W | S |
| Less than 85 | 12.3 | 10.3 | 10.9 | 7.6 | 8.1 | 11.2 | 9.0 | 7.5 | 11.2 | 14.6 | 9.5 |
| 85–95 | 37.2 | 35.9 | 36.8 | 35.8 | 36.9 | 35.1 | 32.2 | 33.5 | 36.1 | 38.9 | 34.7 |
| Greater than 95 | 50.6 | 53.8 | 52.3 | 56.6 | 55.1 | 53.7 | 58.8 | 59.0 | 52.8 | 46.4 | 55.7 |
| | 100.0 | 100.0 | 100.0 | 100.0 | 100.0 | 100.0 | 100.0 | 100.0 | 100.0 | 100.0 | 100.0 |
| N = | 1085 | 662 | 840 | 689 | 736 | 1574 | 537 | 533 | 874 | 488 | 948 |

NW Northern-western; N Northern; EWR East and West Riding; NM North Midlands; E Eastern; LSE London and South East; S Southern; SW South-western; M Midlands; W Wales; S Scotland.

*Table 2b  Regional distribution of mean attendance rates for each social class*

| Social class | Region | | | | | | | | | | |
|---|---|---|---|---|---|---|---|---|---|---|---|
| | NW | N | EWR | NM | E | LSE | S | SW | M | W | S |
| I | 94.2 | 97.2 | 94.7 | 95.2 | 94.7 | 95.4 | 95.2 | 95.3 | 97.0 | 93.6 | 95.5 |
| II | 93.9 | 95.1 | 93.3 | 95.1 | 94.4 | 94.7 | 94.5 | 94.5 | 94.1 | 94.7 | 95.6 |
| III NM | 93.8 | 93.6 | 93.1 | 95.0 | 95.0 | 95.0 | 95.9 | 94.3 | 95.2 | 93.1 | 94.2 |
| III M | 93.3 | 93.4 | 93.0 | 93.5 | 93.5 | 92.5 | 92.8 | 94.1 | 93.1 | 92.2 | 94.4 |
| IV | 90.3 | 93.7 | 92.6 | 94.6 | 92.0 | 91.4 | 93.8 | 94.4 | 92.0 | 91.9 | 93.3 |
| V | 88.9 | 88.6 | 91.3 | 92.0 | 92.2 | 92.1 | 92.0 | 92.1 | 91.2 | 88.2 | 90.2 |

B

the rest of Britain (54 per cent, as opposed to 49 per cent for the rest of Britain and 30 per cent for Scotland), so that these factors can be excluded (DES 1970).

An additional analysis pertinent to these questions is summarized in Table 2b (page 33)), which indicates that even within each social group the regional pattern of attendance is similar to the general one, though the manual/nonmanual dichotomy is more distinct in some (e.g. the north of England) than in others. The present data also reveals that at age eleven the boys in the cohort were better attenders than girls (Table 3a). The difference, though small, is statistically significant. Though this result may seem surprising it is consistent with those of some localized studies of different age groups (e.g. Institute for the Study of the Treatment of Delinquency 1972, Gooch and Pringle 1966). At a national level it also confirms the results of Douglas and Ross (1968) with eleven year olds, though those authors point out that this order is the reverse of that in the early years of schooling. There is some evidence that illnesses of various sorts are more prevalent amongst girls (ISTD 1972) and there is also the possibility that older girls are kept at home more often than boys to help with domestic chores. Table 3b shows that no gross regional variation in this pattern occurs. Table 3c shows moreover that the differential tends to persist across all social groups.

It has been reported by several writers that attendance patterns change from age group to age group. Douglas and Ross (1968) found absence more frequent in the earlier than later years of primary schooling. Clyne (1968) reports that in

---

*Table 3a  Distribution of attendance by sex*

| Attendance rate (%) | Boys | Girls |
|---|---|---|
| Less than 85 | 10.2 | 10.5 |
| 85—95 | 34.5 | 37.2 |
| 95—100 | 55.4 | 52.2 |
| | 100.0 | 100.0 |
| N = | 4653 | 4314 |

---

*Table 3b Regional distribution of mean percentaged attendance rates for boys and girls*

| Region | Boys | Girls |
|--------|------|-------|
| NW  | 92.9 | 91.9 |
| N   | 93.6 | 93.0 |
| EWR | 93.4 | 92.1 |
| NM  | 93.8 | 93.9 |
| E   | 93.4 | 93.9 |
| LSE | 93.1 | 92.7 |
| S   | 93.5 | 93.7 |
| SW  | 94.8 | 93.5 |
| M   | 92.6 | 93.0 |
| W   | 91.9 | 90.9 |
| S   | 93.7 | 93.7 |

*Table 3c Mean percentaged attendance rates: sex by social class*

| Social class | Boys | Girls |
|--------------|------|-------|
| I      | 95.3 | 95.1 |
| II     | 94.7 | 94.3 |
| III NM | 94.3 | 94.6 |
| III M  | 93.5 | 92.9 |
| IV     | 93.1 | 92.0 |
| V      | 90.5 | 90.4 |

Swansea, attendance rates have been found to improve with age (see also Tyerman 1972). Our own data confirm that overall attendance rates improved markedly between the ages of seven and eleven (Table 4). Thus only about half as many of the cohort were poor attenders (less than 85 per cent) at eleven than at seven. However, the improvement is by no means a general one; a more detailed analysis (not shown here) reveals that of the poor attenders at eleven only half were poor attenders at seven. Nor is the improvement a general one across all social groups. Table 5 indicates that it is much higher for children of nonmanual workers than for those of manual workers.

*Table 4  Comparison of attendance rates at 7 and 11*

| Attendance rate at 11 | Attendance rate at 7 | | | |
|---|---|---|---|---|
| | Less than 85% | 85—95% | 95—100% | N = |
| Less than 85% | 24.4 | 9.0 | 4.8 | 919 |
| 85—95% | 44.0 | 39.7 | 29.0 | 3178 |
| 95—100% | 31.7 | 51.4 | 66.2 | 4785 |
| N = | 1459 | 3298 | 3331 | |
| | 100.0% | 100.0% | 100.0% | |

*Table 5  Attendance rates at 7 and 11: social class comparison*

| Attendance rate at 11 | Less than 85% attendance at 7 by social class (percentaged) | | | | | |
|---|---|---|---|---|---|---|
| | I | II | III NM | III M | IV | V |
| Less than 85% | 10.5 | 12.7 | 14.4 | 23.3 | 27.2 | 40.0 |
| 85—95% | 39.4 | 53.4 | 46.7 | 43.2 | 43.5 | 33.0 |
| 95—100% | 50.0 | 33.9 | 38.8 | 33.5 | 29.3 | 27.0 |
| N = | 38 | 189 | 90 | 576 | 239 | 100 |
| | 100.0% | 100.0% | 100.0% | 100.0% | 100.0% | 100.0% |

## The truancy estimates

It is well known that truancy (i.e. illegal absence for whatever reason) accounts for only a small proportion of all absences. Estimates of the magnitude of this proportion vary considerably: Magnay (1959) suggests 0.74 per cent; Bransby (1951) gives a figure of 3.3 per cent; Tyerman (1968) estimates 5 per cent; and Plowden (1966) suggests that only 4 per cent of absentees are truanting. However the real extent of the problem is difficult to define because of the lack of official figures and because of the impossibility of accurately ascertaining what is and is not truancy. Here we describe the incidence of truancy as assessed by teachers' knowledge of the attendance behaviour of each study child. This is supplemented with information regarding some of the personal characteristics and circumstances of the children defined. Our assessment of which of the study children have truanted is taken from the teachers' responses to one of the items in the Bristol Social Adjustment Guide (Stott 1966) which teachers were asked to complete during the second followup. In this item teachers were asked to underline which of certain descriptions applies to the study child in question. Our group of 'truants' is comprised of those children for whom one or more of the following descriptions was underlined:

1  has truanted once or twice
2  has truanted often
3  suspected of truancy.

Such responses, of course, represent the teacher's subjective impression of each child's attendance behaviour and are in no way substitutes for firm, reliable figures. Even so they may serve as a useful complement to data of other sorts collected elsewhere.

Of the total sample of children 14,140 had completed BSAGs. Of these 170 or 1.2 per cent (in the tables which follow the totals sometimes vary slightly from this figure as a small number of children do not have complete information for all the variables considered) were described as having truanted or being suspected of it. There proved to be an appreciable sex differential in these returns: of 170, 127 (74.7 per cent) were boys compared with 51.4 per cent of the whole sample. This prevalence of truanting among boys rather than girls — in contradistinction to the sex differential for overall attendance — is consistent with findings from other sources (Tyerman 1968), and probably reflects the greater tendency for conformist behaviour patterns among girls (Pringle, Butler and Davie 1966).

Turning now to some of the distributions of truancy, Table 6 shows the regional frequencies of children of the study who were described as 'truants'.

*Table 6  Regional distribution of truants*

|  | NE | ME | LSE | SSW | Wales | Scotland |
|---|---|---|---|---|---|---|
| Truants | 48 (1.3%) | 36 (1.0%) | 38 (1.5%) | 13 (0.7%) | 9 (1.2%) | 26 (1.7%) |
| Nontruants | 3757 | 3664 | 2490 | 1778 | 767 | 1462 |

N North England; ME Midlands and East England; LSE London and South East; SSW South and South West.

In so far as these data are an accurate reflection of actual truancy rates, they broadly correspond with the attendance returns, such that high rates of truancy are indicated where high rates of absence are recorded (see Table 1). Scottish children, however, would appear to be an exception, exhibiting a disproportionate frequency of truancy, but these figures are compatible with those of the ISTD Glasgow Survey (ISTD 1972).

Table 7 Social class distribution of 'truants'

|  | Social class | | | | |
|---|---|---|---|---|---|
|  | I & II | III NM | III M | IV | V |
| Truants (%) | .32 | .54 | 1.1 | 1.8 | 3.1 |
| N = | 2861 | 1117 | 5201 | 2000 | 708 |

Table 8 Truancy by number of schools attended

Number of schools attended since age of five

|  | 1 | 2 | 3+ |
|---|---|---|---|
| Truants (%) | .89 | 1.1 | 1.9 |
| N = | 6549 | 4230 | 1991 |

Table 7 presents the incidence of 'truancy' within each social group and confirms the manual/nonmanual dichotomy consistently found by other writers (Tyerman 1968).

It is of course quite possible that these proportions reflect a positive or negative 'halo effect'; teachers might expect working-class children to truant more often and unconsciously introduce bias into their responses on the BSAG. It might be anticipated that children of mobile families, being shifted frequently from school to school, would be less settled in their contemporary institution at any one time and thus exhibit a high proportion of unexplained absences. Table 8 supports this hypothesis, showing that 'truancy' for those who had attended three or more schools by age eleven was described twice as often as those who had only attended one school.

Table 9 compares the proportions of children described as 'truanting' in LEA and in independent schools and reveals the expected trend in favour of the latter, although the numbers are so small that this does not in fact reach statistical significance.

It has long been a matter of conjecture whether or not streaming in primary schools (i.e. grouping by attainment or ability) affects either the attainment or contentedness of the children. The apparent effects of streaming on attainment have produced conflicting findings in research (Plowden 1966, Daniels 1961, Ferri 1971). However, there is more of a consensus over the contentedness and satisfaction of children in streamed or unstreamed schools (Clegg 1963, Daniels 1961, Jackson 1964). As Plowden (1966) puts it, 'Streaming can be wounding to children', and Jackson (1964) describes how, in schools of his survey, unstreamed schools replaced competition by helpfulness and generated a friendly atmosphere in large institutions as well as small ones. Table 10 presents the proportions of children in streamed and unstreamed schools who were described as truants. These data show first that there is little difference in proportions

Table 9 Proportion of children truanting in LEA and independent schools

|  | LEA | Independent |
|---|---|---|
| Truants (%) | 1.3 | .52 |
| N = | 13491 | 582 |

Table 10 Truancy by streaming and nonstreaming streaming

|  | Not streamed | Higher Streamed | Middle | Lower | Total |
|---|---|---|---|---|---|
| Truants | 109 (67.3%) | 8 (4.9%) | 8 (4.9%) | 37 (22.8%) | 100.0% |
| Nontruants | 9255 (67.7%) | 1785 (13.1%) | 1316 (9.6%) | 1315 (9.6%) | 100.0% |

between streamed and nonstreamed schools and secondly that within streamed schools there is disproportionately lower truancy in higher and middle streams and disproportionately higher truancy in lower streams. This could reflect the tendency noted by Plowden (1966) of making trust and responsibility the preserves of certain classes — 'no more certain way could be found of alienating children from school . . . .'

We now turn to consideration of some of the social circumstances of children described as having truanted. Many researchers over the last two or three decades have concluded that of all the factors associated with the attainments and progress of children in school none has more influence than parental encouragement (Fraser 1958, Wiseman 1968). How do the parents of truants in our sample compare with the rest of the population in this respect?

During the second followup all parents of study children were asked at what age they would like their child to leave school. Table 11 shows that the proportion of children described as truanting was some six to seven times higher among parents who wanted their children to leave school as soon as possible, than among those who wanted their children to stay on. This trend was also reflected in the parents expressed wishes regarding the further education or training of their children (Table 12).

*Table 11  Parents desired school-leaving age*

|  | ASAP | Stay on | Don't know |
|---|---|---|---|
| Truants (%) | 4.8 | .69 | 1.8 |
| N = | 687 | 9704 | 2440 |

*Table 12  Parents desire for further education or training*

|  | Yes | No | Don't know |
|---|---|---|---|
| Truants (%) | .90 | 3.3 | 2.0 |
| N = | 10587 | 392 | 1848 |

Parents' spontaneous enquiries concerning the school progress of their children are also a useful index of their interest. Accordingly teachers were asked whether the parents of each study child had ever taken the initative to visit school to discuss these matters. Table 13 shows the percentages of truants' parents who had taken such an initiative compared with those pertaining to the rest of the sample. The proportions actually correspond closely for *either* father or mother; it is only when *both* parents' involvement in such initiatives was recorded that differences between truants and nontruants emerged. The table also indicates that it was more often the case for truants than non-truants that neither parents had taken any such initiative. This disparity in degree of presumptive parental interest was also confirmed when teachers were asked for their impressions of the fathers' concern for study children's education. The percentages falling into each category of degree of interest for truants and nontruants are shown in Table 14.

*Table 13  Parental initiative in making school contacts*

|  | Father | Mother | Both | Neither | Totals |
|---|---|---|---|---|---|
| Truants | 8 (4.8%) | 53 (31.7%) | 16 (9.6%) | 90 (53.9%) | 100.0% |
| Nontruants | 639 (4.7%) | 4300 (31.4%) | 3066 (22.4%) | 5688 (41.5%) | 100.0% |

*Table 14  Father's concern for education*

|  | Overconcerned | Interested | Little interest | Can't say | Total |
|---|---|---|---|---|---|
| Truants | 3 (1.9%) | 37 (23%) | 81 (50.3%) | 40 (24.8%) | 100% |
| Nontruants | 342 (2.6%) | 7143 (54.9%) | 2265 (12.4%) | 3256 (25.0%) | 100% |

Finally, all parents were asked whether or not they had approached any welfare agencies (welfare associations, children's societies, school health service, guidance clinics etc) on behalf of any member of the family. This was found to be the case for 44.7 per cent of parents of truants compared with only 10.7 per cent for parents of nontruants (Table 15).

We now turn to the teachers' impressions of some of the personal characteristics of those study children described as

*Table 15  Referral to agency*

|  | Yes | No | Total |
|---|---|---|---|
| Truants | 71 (44.7%) | 88 (55.3%) | 100.0% |
| Nontruants | 1445 (10.7%) | 12074 (89.3%) | 100.0% |

truants. These data were all collected from items in the educational questionnaire of the second followup. What, for example, do teachers think is the level of scholastic ability among such children? Table 16 presents ratings for several related items. Two facts are strikingly clear: first, the extremely low proportions of truants who were rated above average or even average on these items, and second the remarkable consistency of the proportions across the different areas. The only item for which the majority of truants fall into the average category is oral ability; but even here only 5 per cent of truants are said to be above average; for all other items the vast majority of truants are placed in the 'below average' category. In addition (not shown in Table 16)

*Table 16  Teachers' ratings of aspects of childrens' scholastic abilities*

| Item | Rating | | | |
|---|---|---|---|---|
|  | Above average | Average | Below average | Total |
| *General Knowledge* | | | | |
| Truants | 9 (5.3%) | 41 (24.3%) | 119 (70.4%) | 100% |
| Nontruants | 3584 (25.9%) | 6207 (44.8%) | 4057 (29.3%) | 100% |
| *Number ability* | | | | |
| Truants | 6 (3.6%) | 32 (19.1%) | 130 (77.4%) | 100% |
| Nontruants | 3455 (25.0%) | 5234 (37.9%) | 5129 (37.1%) | 100% |
| *Oral ability* | | | | |
| Truants | 5 (3.0%) | 67 (39.6%) | 97 (57.4%) | 100% |
| Nontruants | 3208 (23.2%) | 7629 (55.1%) | 3006 (21.7%) | 100% |
| *Use of books* | | | | |
| Truants | 9 (5.3%) | 54 (31.9%) | 106 (62.7%) | 100% |
| Nontruants | 4254 (30.7%) | 6474 (46.8%) | 3119 (22.5%) | 100% |

according to teachers' judgments only 12.4 per cent of truants have 'any outstanding ability' compared with 22.1 per cent of nontruants.

There must of course be several factors at work in the teachers' arrival at these ratings; not least of these will be the inevitable negative halo-effect in the teachers' perceptions of truanting children. But we must also bear in mind the poor validity and reliability of the data itself. For example the assessment of oral ability may reflect the teachers' ethno-centric concepts of what constitutes 'good' English (Rosen 1972); what is perceived as 'general knowledge' will tend to be that which corresponds with the substance of the school curriculum; and teachers are unlikely to have accurate insights into the children's use of books outside school.

In view of these figures, it might be expected that relatively fewer truants showed progress in the course of the school year, or conversely that more of them would deteriorate. Indeed, this is borne out by the results presented in Table 17 (teachers' report of progress in the current school year), and is reinforced by the disproportionate numbers of truants said by teachers to be in need of special educational treatment (Table 18).

It might also be expected that school is not a very welcoming or hospitable place for those children with truant tendencies and that they would tend to be seen as disruptive. Teachers were asked whether or not the study children in their schools displayed any serious weaknesses or drawbacks

*Table 17 Progress in school*

|  | Improvement | No change | Deterioration | Can't say | Total |
|---|---|---|---|---|---|
| Truants | 71 (42.5%) | 81 (48.5%) | 12 (7.2%) | 3 (1.8%) | 100% |
| Nontruants | 7056 (51.4%) | 6288 (45.8%) | 193 (1.4%) | 188 (1.4%) | 100% |

*Table 18 Need for special educational treatment*

|  | Would benefit | Would not | Can't say | Total |
|---|---|---|---|---|
| Truants | 24 (15.0%) | 121 (75.6%) | 15 (9.4%) | 100% |
| Nontruants | 252 (1.9%) | 13155 (96.4%) | 243 (1.8%) | 100% |

of character. 'Delinquency', 'outgoing' and 'easily led' traits were, according to their reports, severalfold more common amongst truants than nontruants (Table 19).

Finally, in this section, the study children themselves were asked to what extent they enjoyed their spare time. Truants gave more extreme responses to this question, a greater proportion of them saying that they always enjoyed their spare time, but also proportionately more saying that they were often bored (Table 20).

*Attendance and school attainment*
In the context of scholastic development, it is clearly worth asking how far frequent absence is associated with the attainments of children in school. This is all the more important since few previous studies in this country have explicitly examined this association. Douglas and Ross (1968) remind us that the shorter school year of independent school pupils, and of pupils in the USA, suggests that within wide limits the actual amount of time spent in school has little effect on the attainments of children. Nor, seemingly, is the amount of time available for homework related to school achievement as judged by the sustained academic progress of pupils who do part-time jobs (Newsom 1963). However, relatively high attainment scores and high attendance rates tended to go together in a followup study of children who had been in either 'progressive' or 'traditional' primary schools (Gooch and Pringle 1966) and results already pub-

*Table 19  Behavioural traits*

|  | None | Delinquency | Outgoing | Easily led | Total |
|---|---|---|---|---|---|
| Truants | 108 (63.5%) | 13 (7.6%) | 39 (22.9%) | 10 (5.9%) | 100% |
| Nontruants | 13082 (93.6%) | 34 (0.2%) | 568 (4.1%) | 286 (2.1%) | 100% |

*Table 20  Enjoyment of spare time*

|  | Always enjoy | Sometimes bored | Often bored |
|---|---|---|---|
| Truants | 65 (43.6%) | 71 (47.6%) | 13 (8.7%) |
| Nontruants | 4163 (30.9%) | 8816 (65.5%) | 477 (3.5%) |

lished by the National Child Development Study showed that by the age of seven those children who started school a term earlier than their peers were significantly ahead in their attainment (Pringle, Butler and Davie 1966).

Here we compare the attendance rates of the group of children referred to in the first section of this chapter with their scores on three types of standardized attainment tests:

1 A reading comprehension test, a parallel version of the Watts-Vernon Test specially constructed by the National Foundation for Educational Research for use in our second followup.
2 An arithmetic/mathematics test also constructed by the NFER for our purposes.
3 A general ability test similarly provided by the NFER.

All of these tests were standardized and validated in the usual fashion on children of ten to eleven years prior to use. The mean scores for the whole cohort were as follows:

1 Reading comprehension 16.6
2 Arithmetic/mathematic 17.6
3 General ability 43.7

It is, of course, necessary to make several qualifications about the meaning of such scores before considering the data. For example, all reading test items will inevitably reflect, in style and grammatical structure, the 'standard English' of the test designers — a language which working-class children, moving in a linguistically and culturally disparate context, will not be so familiar with (Rosen 1972). A test score does not reflect absolute verbal competence, nor the *capacity* for reading. For perhaps the majority of working class children reading materials in schools are not the familiar context which trigger 'the children's imaginings' and 'are not triggers on the children's curiosity and explorations in his family and community' (Bernstein 1970). Similar criticisms can be made of arithmetic tests; culturally-determined differences of cognitive strategy, while having equal utility in any real-life context, may not be equally reflected in the abstract context of test items (Ginsberg 1970). General ability scores can be criticized on a variety of grounds, notably their lack of clear definition (Vernon 1968, Gillham 1973). their dubious validity (McClelland 1973, Ryan 1972) and their cultural bias (Houghton and Richardson 1973). In sum attainment test scores will tend to reflect, like school achievement in general, the cultural (i.e. linguistic, cognitive, dispositional etc) identity between the child and the school system. They must not be thought of as ratings of any *absolute* learning capacity; the same cultural identity/disparity is likely to be responsible in large measure for *both* school progress and affinity for school (i.e. attendance rates): the one cannot be thought of as *causing* the other.

With this in mind, then, we turn first of all to the reading comprehension scores presented in Table 21. These data reveal that there appears to be little relationship between test scores and attendance rates for the children in nonmanual groups (the score for the group III NM with <85 per cent attendance is likely to be an aberration due to the inordinately small number of children in this group (36); the score is within the standard error of a figure compatible with that of the remaining children in this group, and this applies to the arithmetic and general ability test scores for the same children, given below). It is only when we look at the data for the children of manual groups and especially group V that a significant relationship emerges. The results also show that among the manual groups the children with less than 85 per cent attendance rates have particularly low reading scores. A very similar picture emerges with both the arithmetic (Table 22) and general ability (Table 23) test scores. This preliminary analysis would seem to show an association between attendance rates and school attainment. They are also in agreement with the results of Douglas and Ross (1968) who found among eleven year olds in the National Survey a significant relationship between attendance and composite test scores for children of lower social groups but not those of the upper middle classes.

Table 21 *Attendance and mean reading comprehension scores*

| Social class | Attendance | | |
| --- | --- | --- | --- |
| | < 85% | 85—95% | 95—100% |
| I | 19.8 | 19.8 | 20.2 |
| II | 18.2 | 18.7 | 19.2 |
| III NM | 14.3 | 17.5 | 18.6 |
| III M | 13.0 | 15.1 | 15.7 |
| IV | 12.5 | 14.3 | 14.4 |
| V | 9.8 | 12.5 | 13.8 |

Table 22  Attendance and mean arithmetic/mathematic scores

| Social class | Attendance | | |
|---|---|---|---|
| | < 85% | 85—95% | 95—100% |
| I | 22.6 | 22.7 | 24.4 |
| II | 19.2 | 21.2 | 22.7 |
| III NM | 12.2 | 19.3 | 21.1 |
| III M | 10.3 | 14.9 | 16.5 |
| IV | 9.5 | 13.4 | 14.6 |
| V | 7.3 | 11.0 | 13.7 |

*An overview*
The data from the National Child Development Study summarized in this chapter provide factual answers to some outstanding questions; but they inevitably raise many more. We have provided evidence of the attendance rates prevalent in certain groups; of some of the personal attributes, parental interests and social class origins of those whom teachers described as 'truants'; and of the association between attendance and school attainment. Such evidence, in common with that from a variety of sources, points inexorably to the location of the overwhelming proportion of absenteeism

Table 23  Attendance and mean general ability scores

| Social class | Attendance | | |
|---|---|---|---|
| | < 85% | 85—95% | 95—100% |
| I | 51.1 | 52.7 | 53.5 |
| II | 46.1 | 50.1 | 51.0 |
| III NM | 34.3 | 46.0 | 48.9 |
| III M | 34.4 | 40.7 | 42.8 |
| IV | 32.7 | 39.1 | 39.7 |
| V | 26.8 | 32.3 | 38.3 |

among children of the working class. Thus Plowden (1966) (interpreting the overall figures of their own survey) lamented the frequent absence of a relatively small group of children: 12—20 per cent of children were found to be absent for a sixth of the time they should have been in school.

Absence from school is undoubtedly a multicausal phenomenon. Its aetiological spectrum ranges from active withdrawal (e.g. to help at home) to those conditions, forms of truancy and 'school phobia', often placed in a quasi-pathological perspective (e.g. Clyne 1968, Kahn and Nursten 1967).

The explanation of the phenomenon is a formidable task, embedded as it is in a web of seeming contradictions. Thus Newsom (1963) presented examples of some of the most rundown, disadvantaged 'slum' schools in their survey which had attendance rates exceeding 93—94 per cent, a tribute to the teachers concerned; and Hargreaves (1966) describes how the emergence of a flourishing 'delinquescent' culture in lower forms of secondary schools can boost attendance rates, but for the opposite reasons of those intended by the school. We have already mentioned the consistent difficulties experienced by authorities wishing to improve attendance rates. For the vast majority of nonpathological absentees, therefore, the problem still clearly demands some sort of perspective.

Tyerman (1972) suggests that a 'sense of purpose' in the school felt by parents, teachers and pupils is the single most powerful influence on school attendance. Wedge and Prosser (1973), referring to disadvantaged (i.e. absentee-prone) groups, ask for how many such children is school really relevant, 'Education as a social distributor of life chances often compounds rather than eases the difficulties.' Thus absenteeism of the degree consistently encountered may project a considerable irony when seen in the context of that same address by W. E. Forster a century ago. He concluded with the words 'To its honour, Parliament has lately decided that England shall in future be governed by popular government. I am one of those who would not wait until the people are educated before entrusting them with political power.' It can indeed be argued that for a substantial proportion of the population, education as it is, has had the opposite effect of that intended, compounding the sense of inferiority and subordination, encouraging the relinquishment of responsibility, and suppressing the 'sense of purpose' of which Tyerman speaks (Richardson 1974, Rowe 1970, Squibb 1973). If this is indeed the case it presents a challenge for both the analytic and creative powers of educators and social scientists everywhere.

*Acknowledgments*
The research described in this chapter was supported by grants from the Department of Education and Science, and the Department of Health and Social Security and the Social Science Research Council. This is gratefully acknowledged. A project on the scale of the National Child Development Study inevitably involves the contribution of many individuals; we thank past and present members of the research team who have contributed to the collection and treatment of the data described here. We also thank members of staff of the National Children's Bureau for their comments and criticisms.

*References*

BAKER, J. (1964) *Children in Chancery* London: Hutchinson
BERNSTEIN, B. (1970) 'Education cannot compensate for society' in R. Rubenstein and C. Stoneman (Eds) *Education for Democracy* Harmondsworth: Penguin
BRANSBY E. R. (1951) A study of absence from school *Medical Officer* 86, 223 and 237.
BUTLER, N. R. and BONHAM, D. G. (1963) *Perinatal Mortality* London and Edinburgh: Livingstone
BUTLER, N. R. and ALBERMAN, E. D. (1969) *Perinatal Problems* London and Edinburgh: Livingstone
CLEGG, A. B. (1963) 'Childrens' attitudes to streaming' in B. Simon (Ed) *Nonstreaming in the Junior School* Leicester: PSW Publications
CLYNE M. B. (1966) *Absent* London: Tavistock
CURTIS, S. J. (1967) *History of Education in Great Britain* London: University Tutorial Press

DANIELS, J. C. (1961) Effects of streaming in the primary school *British Journal of Educational Psychology* 31, 69—78 and 119—126

DAVIE, R., BUTLER, N. R. and GOLDSTEIN, H. (1972) *From Birth to Seven* London: Longmans

DES (1971) *Statistics of Education 1970 Volume 1 Schools* London: HMSO

DES (1967) *Children and their Primary Schools* (Plowden Report) London: HMSO

DOUGLAS, J. W. B. (1964) *The Home and the School* London: MacGibbon and Kee

DOUGLAS, J. W. B. and ROSS, J. M. (1965) The effects of absence on primary school performance *British Journal of Educational Research* 38, 28—40

FERRI, E. (1971) *Streaming: Two Years Later* Slough: NFER

FRASER, E. (1959) *Home Environment and the School* London: University of London Press

GILLHAM, J. (1973) The British Intelligence Scale for Children *Bulletin of the British Psychological Society* (in press)

GINSBERG, H. (1972) *The Myth of the Deprived Child* New Jersey: Prentice Hall

GOOCH, S. and PRINGLE, M. L. K. (1966) *Four Years on* London: Longman

HARGREAVES D. (1966) *Social Relations in a Secondary School* London: Routledge and Kegan Paul

HOUGHTON, V. P. and RICHARDSON, K. (1973) Race and IQ *New Humanist* September

INSTITUTE FOR THE STUDY AND TREATMENT OF DELINQUENCY (1972) *Report by Working Party on Truancy* (unpublished)

JACKSON, B. (1964) *Streaming: An Educational System in Miniature* London: Routledge and Kegan Paul.

KAHN, J. H. and NURSTEN, J. D. (1968) *Unwillingly to School* Oxford: Pergamon

MCCLELLAND, D. (1973) Testing for competence rather than for 'intelligence' *American Psychologist*

MACLURE, J. S. (1967) *Educational Documents* London: Methuen

MAGNAY, H. S. (1959) in *Truancy or School Phobia?* Proceedings of the fifteenth interclinic conference London: National Association for Mental Health Muller

MINISTRY OF EDUCATION (1963) *Half Our Future* (Newsom Report) London: HMSO

PRINGLE, M. L. K., BUTLER, N. R. and DAVIE, R. (1966) *11,000 Seven Year Olds* London: Longman

RANKIN, L. (1961) Irregular attendance at school *Educational Review* 13, 121—7

RICHARDSON K. (1974) 'The institutional mythology' in V. P. Houghton and K. Richardson (Eds) *Recurrent Education* London: Ward Lock Educational

ROSEN, H. (1972) *Language and Class* Bristol: Falling Wall Press

ROWE, A. (1970) 'Primary schools' in R. Rubinstein and C. Stoneman (Eds) *Education for Democracy* Harmondsworth: Penguin

RYAN, J. (1972) 'The illusion of objectivity' in K. Richardson, D. Spears and M. P. R. Richardson (Eds) *Race, Culture and Intelligence* Harmondsworth: Penguin

STOTT, D. H. (1973) *The Social Adjustment of Children: Manual to Bristol Social Adjustment Guide* London: University of London Press

SQUIBB, D. G. (1973) Education and class *Educational Research* 15, 3, 194—208

TAYLOR G. and SAUNDERS, T. B. (1965) *The New Law of Education* London: Butterworth

TENNENT, S. A. (1971) School nonattendance and delinquency *Educational Research* 13, 3, 185—190

TYERMAN, M. J. (1968) *Truancy* London: University of London Press

TYERMAN, M. J. (1972) 'Absent from school' *Trends in Education* London: DES

VERNON, P. E. (1968) What is potential ability? *Bulletin of the British Psychological Society* 21, 211—219

WEDGE, P. and PROSSER, H. (1973) *Born to Fail?* London: Arrow Books

WEST, E. G. (1965) *Education and the State* London: Institute of Economic Affairs

WISEMAN, S. (1968) *Intelligence and Ability* Harmondsworth: Penguin

*Rhodes Boyson*

# The need for realism

There is a conspiracy of silence over truancy from schools as there is about violence in schools, and practising teachers and concerned parents have learnt to treat the official figures with scepticism. High truancy figures cast doubt upon the efficiency of a school, a local education authority or even the national system of state education itself. It is not therefore surprising that the educational establishment does not warm towards anyone rash enough to ask for figures of school attendance. Nor does any headmaster wish to discredit his own school or hazard his own promotion prospects, and education officials do not welcome questions asked by elected committee members.

Over the last few years I have kept a special file on truancy figures and there seems little doubt that these are increasing and that something like 500,000 children are playing truant from school every day, if truancy is taken to exclude all forms of voluntary nonsickness, nonfamily holiday or crisis absence from school but includes casual absences taken with parental connivance.

The secretary of the National Association of Chief Welfare Officers has said that some 5 per cent of school-children — 500,000 in number — played truant every week even before the raising of the minimum school leaving age to sixteen in September 1973. The president of the same organization is on record as estimating that 420,000 children played truant in early 1973 at any one time, a figure I consider an underestimate. A year earlier Dr L. W. White, general secretary of the National Association of Divisional

Executives, estimated that truancy figures rose as high as 10 per cent over the country as a whole.

One in five children has been listed as absent at any one time in Salford, one in ten in Liverpool and one in twelve in London and Devon. If genuine sickness and special causes absence is taken as 5 per cent, then truancy could be 15 per cent of all children in Salford, 5 per cent in Liverpool and 7–8 per cent in London and Devon. These are high figures but since the London figures point to twice as many fourth as first year children being absent in secondary schools, most absence is obviously voluntary and does not arise from sickness.

As long ago as December 1970 Edwin Noble told the NUT Educational Conference that about one in four Manchester schoolchildren was absent sometime in each week, and that the average Manchester schoolchild lost a full year of his period of compulsory school attendance through absence. There are schools where attendance has dropped to below 75 per cent, 65 per cent or even 50 per cent over a month or even a year. One London comprehensive school has a published attendance figure of 67 per cent for a full year.

All these figures predate the raising of the minimum school leaving age and it has been estimated that since then truancy in many secondary schools has increased by 50 per cent. This so-called reform which cost the country some £133,000,000 a year was supported by all political parties, but opposed by the majority of teachers in contact with the fifteen year olds. Mr John Gordon, retiring deputy headmaster of Sir Philip Magnus School, Islington, said in November 1973 that teachers had been turned into jailors by the raising of the school leaving age, a sad if even partially true statement.

Since in 1970 1,200 fifteen year old and 5,000 sixteen year old girls gave birth to babies, one wonders if such mothers will be classed as voluntary or involuntary truants. It is not generally realized that the minimum school leaving age is now effectively 16 years 8 months for many children and the pupils allowed to leave on their birthdays account for far less than 1 per cent of their age group. A girl who becomes sixteen on September 3rd will not be able to leave until she is 16 years 7 months the following April, almost old enough to have children within the marriage bond. Will her husband or her parents be prosecuted for her nonattendance at school?

Figures of attendance already quoted refer to those marked present on registers. The August 1973 issue of *Where?* threw serious doubt on the reliability of such figures and it is becoming more widely recognized that all pupils who register at 9 am may not still be in school at 10 am or even 9.30 am. Huge new city comprehensive schools with low railings and many gates, ineffectiveness of teachers in keeping discipline, continued lesson changes and walks of up to ten minutes between classrooms encourage casual truancy.

It would be interesting to ascertain whether two out of three of our fifteen year old schoolchildren were actually present in our schools at any time, whatever the registers might indicate. It might also be a useful idea to return to an earlier method whereby the visiting chairmen of governors actually checked the registers of all classes against the pupils present when they visited their schools, and woe betide the teacher whose register was inaccurate. The demand by teachers for professional freedom and lack of supervision has led to an all-round decline in standards. Perhaps Her Majesty's inspectors might be sent to spotcheck registers. Senior clerks from education offices now examine a head's Form Seven return, on which his salary and the special responsibility allowances of his staff are calculated, and it is only one step further to an examination of class registers of attendance by some outsider.

There is little doubt that many teachers are very willing to ignore the absence of boys who make their lives a misery and disrupt a class. The 'Nelson touch' in schoolmastering now means turning a blind eye to the absence of boys whose presence is unwelcome! It is this situation of the quiet exclusion of boys which presumably led to the alleged preparation of a confidential letter from Mr Ashley Bramall, the leader of the Inner London Education Authority, referring to the number of 'banned' pupils whose absence from school was unofficial but whose parents had been asked to keep them at home. Mr Bramall said, 'What worried us was the way in some schools that children just disappear from classes without the head telling us or the governors. A few heads may just tell the parents they don't want a child back in school.' Such situations arise in schools where head-teachers and teaching staff cannot rely on the support of governing bodies in suspending pupils, which happens all too often. The Inner London Education Authority sets the tone by claiming that the appeals procedure of parents to governors 'is a reconciliation procedure, not a quasijudicial one'. Yet teachers need help and support not criticism.

It is interesting to find out what boys and girls do when they play truant from school. Some get jobs and are usefully if temporarily employed — unloading lorries, pushing trolleys in markets, working as butchers' helps, or as farmhands. Some stay at home and decorate the house, or build motorcycles like one boy at Kidderminster. Some even listen to school radio broadcasts and watch school programmes on television — in certain cases under more peaceful conditions than they would experience at school. Maybe there is a case for an 'Open School' television series for truants with set examinations and certificates like the Open University, with children being allowed to remain at home if they achieve standards accepted as reasonable for their age and intelligence. This method of a boy or girl achieving high qualifications without attending school will become more important if discipline deteriorates further and good pupils stay at home for their own safety.

The present risk is that many absentees who do not obtain unofficial jobs will drift into delinquency. A boy who first steps out of school pretending he has left his tie or homework at home or his mother wants her house key back, may find absence easier than lessons and begin to frequent the sleazier cafes with his friends until he takes to shoplifting and petty crime. The Chief Constable of Birmingham has commented that the number of children playing truant from school was responsible for a sharp rise in shoplifting by juveniles in that city during school hours. High figures for permanent truants could mean that we are producing a new subcriminal unemployable class worthy of the pen of Dickens. Boys who play truant continuously and defy the law successfully for a number of years are unlikely to become reliable workmen and they could be the source of a large new criminal class which could threaten further the fabric of our society.

A country like ours which continues to pass more and more laws, many, like those on school attendance, unenforced, threatens to destroy obedience to basic law. Nor will truancy be solved by police or court action, except in isolated cases. It takes so long to get a fourth and fifth year boy into court for nonattendance and the fines are so low that many schoolmasters wonder if such action is worthwhile. Nor do many educational authorities welcome such public evidence of the failure of their schools to enforce attendance. Birmingham magistrates asked in January 1974 why a boy had been out of schooling for eleven months.

There have been a number of recent attempts to involve the police more actively in antitruancy drives. In October 1973 the Glasgow police had an eighteen-man special truancy patrol and a month earlier the east London police were asked by ILEA to check up on all youths and girls who looked as if they should be attending school. The education welfare officers do what they can, but their effectiveness seems to have declined as school support, psychological and educational services and home tuition have increased. The misplaced sympathy for, and the emphasis on, the interests of the offender and not the victim or the law has weakened the power of the education welfare officers as it has threatened all law enforcement or even the existence of law itself.

The increase in truancy has gone hand in hand with the schools' retreat from their primary task of schooling. Pupils know that the emphasis on 'liberation', 'social orientation' and 'life-enhancement' has little relevance to them and is simply a means whereby their teachers act out their own frustrations. Thus the children disillusioned by school, walk through the school-gates to the real open school – the outside world. A new generation of schoolmasters and mistresses often concerned with social egalitarianism if not revolution has nothing to offer them. Ordinary boys and their parents know that schools are for schooling and they see little point in attending schools which cease to offer it.

The 1968 *Young School Leavers* report from the Schools Council shows clearly that the working-class boys and girls and their parents rank school subjects by their value in preparing pupils for their work in the outside world. Girls, despite the frenzied efforts of women's liberation, also rate subjects according to how they will help them in being successful wives and mothers. According to *Young School Leavers* the boys – all fifteen year old school leavers – rank mathematics as the most useful school subject with a score of

93 per cent, followed by English with 90 per cent, and metalwork and engineering with 71 per cent. Current affairs and social studies only score 56 per cent and music 8 per cent. The fifteen year old girl leavers put English first with 94 per cent, mathematics second with 92 per cent, housecraft third with 91 per cent and commercial subjects fourth with 81 per cent. The score declines to 29 per cent for history and 11 per cent for music.

The early leavers' parents agree with these judgments of the useful school subjects. The boys' parents list English and mathematics joint first with 91 per cent, and engineering third with 71 per cent. Enthusiasm falls to 45 per cent for current affairs and social studies and 24 per cent for music, and art and crafts. The girls' parents put domestic science first with 92 per cent, English second with 90 per cent and mathematics third with 86 per cent while art and crafts score only 28 per cent and science 24 per cent.

So both children and their parents clearly see schools as institutions which give a boy or girl a chance of a better job and also make the girls better wives and mothers. This is not surprising since education is and always has been largely vocational. Latin in the Middle Ages was studied as the way into the universities and the professions of law, medicine and the Church. O and A level GCEs and good CSEs open doors to better-paid jobs and the universities increase the potential earning power of their graduates. Parents and boys know this, and they recognize too that the best preparation for leisure is to be able to earn enough money to afford it! This is why people came into the factories in the Industrial Revolution, why many work on production lines now and why shorter working weeks are likely to lead to men taking two jobs to increase their earnings. So to the normal pupil and his parents school is basically a preparation for life and a place to be taught the 3Rs, a body of knowledge, disciplined habits of work and vocational skills. No wonder that teachers and schools with other values and little contact with the outside world drive pupils to truancy.

Many suggestions for new courses for ROSLA point to the fact that many teachers and authorities still do not realize the need to make schools 'relevant' to the real world of pupils. Grimsby has 'cosmetology', there are 'personal relationships' in Birkenhead and Cheshire and 'residential experience' in

Wolverhampton, the Isle of Wight and Inner London. The ultimate farce in the retreat from schooling is to open adventure playgrounds for truants and to pretend that they are a substitute for school. If local education authorities cannot enforce school attendance then schooling should be made voluntary and local education authorities disbanded as inefficient bureaucracies. It was first suggested in Camden that pupils 'attending' adventure playgrounds should be marked present in their school registers. Many pupils there have also been in 'attendance' at 'antiauthoritarian' schools run by squatters in old houses taught by teachers who cannot face the classrooms, the structure, and what both they and the kids would call the 'authoritarian' nature of state education! It is not beyond the madness of our age that public money will be given to such disruptive 'schools'.

The ILEA has considered making a teacher and suitable materials and equipment available so that some form of continuing education may be provided for adventure centres. The sending of a teacher to the Christchurch Gardens Adventure Playground in Spitalfields, Stepney where twenty truants were normally in attendance was discussed in the autumn of 1973. Thus the authority which put its face against all selection now introduces a new selection — presumably academic schooling in schools and some leisure form of schooling in adventure playgrounds which will be far less effective than the education provided in the old elementary schools and secondary modern schools in the city centre. The wheel would then come full circle at a lower level as in so much of our modern living.

Christopher Price, late Labour Parliamentary Private Secretary to a Secretary of State for Education and Science, is even on record as saying, 'It is possible that the child would get a better education in a youth club or adventure playground than at a school he doesn't want to go to.' Against such a background each school must attempt to maintain its own standards of school attendance. This is what is done at Highbury Grove. Parental involvement is essential and every parent is seen some three times before his son enters the school. Parents are told of the benefits of regular school attendance and asked to cooperate fully with the school. Every parent is expected to let the school know immediately every time a boy is legitimately absent. By 9.30

in the morning housemasters will be contacting any parent whose boy is absent without reason. Each housemaster has a telephone number for each parent — his home, a neighbour, a relative like his 'nan', the corner shop, his work place. Thus apart from very hard cases boys learn that they cannot escape detection and regular attendance becomes a habit which is easy to maintain.

Random checks on the attendance at lessons ensure that the number of boys who slip out after registration is nil, or minimal. The whole school is checked one lesson a week by senior staff visiting each classroom and checking boys present against the class registers of the teachers and reporting all absentees for whatever apparent reason to their housemasters. The housemasters then check those listed as absent against their genuine absentees. Originally some twelve to fifteen out of 1,300 boys would have disappeared after registration, but it is now rare to find more than one or two boys so absent in the whole school, and occasionally none are absent without the knowledge of their housemasters. The price of high attendance is regular if not eternal vigilance.

It is also important to reward and praise attendance — good discipline and habits arise from a skilled mixture of the carrot and the whip and one without the other is only temporarily effective. One school in Oakland, California, USA, gives 100 trading stamps for a full week's attendance and a bonus of 500 stamps at the end of a term, and at Highbury Grove we present special certificates on prize evenings to all boys who complete one hundred per cent attendance for a year. House attendances are regularly referred to, tutor group attendance charts displayed in house rooms and all tutor groups obtaining 100 per cent attendance in any week are listed in assembly and given a half-hour off school the following week in 'controlled truancy'. Thus an atmosphere of regular attendance is encouraged and we hope to keep up this record despite the difficulties associated with the raising of the school leaving age and the reduced enthusiasm of staff to see the attendance of fifteen to sixteen year old boys who resent a further year in school compared with earning a living in the world outside.

It is very likely that the conjunction of schools retreating from schooling, the raising of the school leaving age, the erosion of school discipline by a vague permissiveness and increased teacher militancy will bring a crisis in all urban schools. The decision of the National Union of Teachers in London in autumn 1973 not to cover lessons for the absences of nonappointed teachers and sick teachers after three days will inevitably increase truancy, since children excluded for one half day from school per week will exclude themselves on other days. Although this is not the intention of the teachers, this action could well be a final blow to urban state schooling. It will certainly further intensify the pressure for caring parents to attempt to afford to leave London or to pay independent school fees for their children where their full-time education is guaranteed or indeed taken for granted. It is one further sign of city breakdown, since in small communities where teachers and parents know one another it is unlikely that teachers would so prejudice their close relationships in the community.

Urban schooling, or indeed all state schooling, will only return to sanity in this country when a reduction in the minimum school leaving age is linked with some form of minimum achievement level being reached before such release is granted. There is no reason why at the age of fourteen, fifteen or sixteen a boy should not sit a school *leaving* certificate and provided he has reached a minimum standard in English, mathematics and a reasonable standard of knowledge in all other subjects, has 95 per cent attendance for the previous three years and a job to go to should not leave school immediately.

In 1861 the Commissioners appointed to look into the state of popular education in England advised, 'The sooner we get rid of the idea that all the education of our people must necessarily be given before people go out to work the better.' Life-long as against terminal education would allow the fourteen year old to leave and come back later when he was freshly motivated for general or vocational education. One thing is certain — many boys would be more advanced in the basic skills and school knowledge at the age of fourteen than they are now at sixteen if there was an earlier way out. The C stream ability boys of our secondary modern and comprehensive schools would be taking truck loads of books home every evening if there was an earlier job ticket available given reasonable achievement. Once again education would be useful and terminal.

There is nothing sacred about a school leaving age of sixteen and one responsible body, the Association of Assistant Masters, asked in January 1974 for official permission to allow troublesome boys to leave early. New Zealand, which has a school leaving age of fifteen, reduced it in 1973 so that a boy or girl can leave at any age with the agreement of his parents, his teachers and his school guidance officers. Italy has a school leaving age of fourteen and Holland of fourteen and a half. In Italy it is even estimated that 25—30 per cent of pupils cease to attend school before they are thirteen years old. France is also considering reducing her minimum school leaving age to fourteen from the age of sixteen to which it was raised in 1959. China has also reduced its period of compulsory schooling to a length of nine to ten years only.

If it is argued, despite the continued changes of party and government policies, that we cannot immediately reverse the raising of our minimum school leaving age, I suggest some immediate alternative improvements. An apprenticeship at the age of fourteen or fifteen could count as continued school attendance and boys' time in the armed services could also count as school attendance. Such amendments would at least indicate that educational levitation and blind man's bluff was at last coming to an end and reality and sanity and true compassion for the academically least-gifted was returning.

*Frank Harris*

# Rebels with a cause

Some time ago I faced a third year class in a secondary modern school. For me it was a new appointment; for them it was just another new teacher. On the second day, Bill, a tousled haired fourteen year old on the front row demanded 'How long you staying sir?' I replied with false confidence, 'Oh I'm permanent' at which Bill grinned and retorted 'they all say that'. It was, after all, said with some justification for his class had had seven form masters in two years. I wasn't surprised to find that Bill was in the habit of taking days off. For him fishing in the Avon was a much more enjoyable and profitable way of spending his schooldays than the struggle to learn which the classroom presented to him. His reading ability was poor and he could only just string the odd sentence together in a badly written composition exercise. But, get him talking to the class about fishing and he became bright, animated and informed.

Derek, in a second year form, spent his afternoons off in town and was frequently picked up near the local bookie. He couldn't read, write or even spell his own name but he could tell you how much you stood to win on the most complicated odds on the day's racing card. He lived on a farm and whenever the harvest or sowing season was upon us we knew that Derek would develop a 'cold' which seemed to be improved, so the school attendance officer told us, by fresh air. A colleague, who came from a farming family, assured me that such was Derek's skill with a tractor that he could have won any ploughing competition in the county. I passed the family farm some years after he had left school and there he was, enthroned on his beloved tractor, chugging down the field. He stopped to hail me with a delightful happy smile lighting up his face. 'I still can't write, sir,' he shouted, and before I could make an appropriate reply he added, 'but me wife can!'

I've often thought about those two boys and how the system failed for them or how they learnt to beat it. They both continued to play truant until the day they left school, despite the considerable efforts of the staff to interest and help them. The world outside was where they wanted to be and, mercifully, they were spared the extra year which the raising of the school leaving age brought. But how many Bills and Dereks are there throughout the country today who are unwilling conscripts in our schools because of the politicians 'promised land'? There were sighs of relief in many staff-rooms when the Labour government, on economic grounds, postponed the raising of the leaving age.

This is not to condemn the tremendous amount of work and initiative that has gone into the design of new curricula for the extra year, or the plans for purpose-built extensions designed to accommodate the ROSLA pupils. But many children were already staying on voluntarily — in some parts of the country as many as 80 per cent. Shouldn't we have encouraged this process rather than statutorily compelled attendance until sixteen?

1974 presented a crisis for many of our secondary schools, particularly in the large cities like Birmingham and London. Some children are already attending schools on a part-time basis (legal truants), or are facing yet another 'supply' teacher. Some subjects are particularly short of teachers; the previous Secretary of State for Education and Science believed she could relieve this shortage by waiving the professional training requirement for science and mathematics teachers, but there have been the gravest warnings from the teaching profession against this. Many of us involved in the training of teachers believe that one year to convert a graduate into a qualified teacher is too short, and the thought of no training at all takes us back into a bleak age. In such circumstances it is not surprising that we have rebels in our schools, children who play truant, disrupt classes and generally resort to hooliganism. Overworked teachers, faced with large classes in difficult conditions, often serving their probationary year, are no match for them.

All headmasters of secondary schools know in their hearts what a problem they have after the conclusion of fifth-year examinations in the early part of the summer term. In this case many of the trouble makers are already sixteen, but must stay at school until the last day of the school term although their formal work is finished. A delegate to the Assistant Masters Association annual conference in Nottingham in January 1974 declared that the weeks of July were three very expensive and difficult weeks if schools had nothing to offer these reluctant pupils. Up to a quarter of the leavers rejected the whole system and damaged property, played truant and swore at women teachers. Another delegate at the same conference gave a picture of the sort of pupil he wanted to get out of school — dressed in 'bovver' boots, jeans and short-sleeved shirts, and with a record of criminal offences. 'They don't even speak English, they just grunt. They will arrive at school and say in effect "keep me amused".'? He added that 'it is not our place to entertain pupils who have no interest in school.'

Mr G. B. C. Palmer, Headmaster of Mark Hall Comprehensive School, Harlow, Essex took up the theme when he wrote in a letter to *The Times* on January 16th 1974:

> Reluctant sixteen year old members of our fifth forms create problems in two ways. They are a problem to us in school because they are unwilling and, dare I say it, unwanted by some teachers. But they also are a greater problem to themselves directly, to us indirectly, when they are out of school. Many of them are.
>
> I would think that anything up to twenty-five (10 per cent) of this age group at this school are almost always absent, with no reason. The authority is apparently powerless to enforce their attendance. They are on the school registers, their places are empty. Numbered amongst the absentees is a married sixteen year old woman with a child.
>
> Some have found occasional illicit employment, and there are many who are just absent, lounging about at home, listening to records, or 'on the loose'. Opportunities for slacking and mischief abound. I doubt whether after these casual months of indolence they will really want to work when they legally may. The law and the educational system are being held in disrespect, and this

is spreading to those who come because they are 'supposed' to come, and indeed to those who come with purpose.

Let no starry-eyed educationist or politician talk of devising 'child-centred' courses and appealing to their 'interests'. A Certificate of Secondary Education has no appeal for at least 15 per cent of our child population. These young people know they should be at work. At present they are not, and the consequences will create problems for society and perhaps disaster for themselves.

Speaking at a College of Preceptors seminar for teachers at Rotherham in November 1973, I expressed sentiments similar to those of Mr Palmer when commenting upon the case of the boys at an Ellesmere Port secondary school in Cheshire, who became so difficult that staff refused to teach them; eventually they were taught in a small group by one teacher. While I agreed that this was an answer to the immediate problem, I went on to ask why rebels should be allowed to disrupt our schools when what many of them needed was the discipline of a job in the outside world. My remarks were subsequently reported in the press and broadcast in BBC news bulletins and I was surprised at the response. Teachers and parents all over the country either wrote to me or telephoned to offer support for my 'campaign' as they put it. An adult education tutor wrote that 'ROSLA has not been one of the wisest decisions, as I've always suspected that it was more a labour market thing than a true educational need.'

Another head wrote a most moving letter in which he pointed out:

We are increasingly confronted by the idiotic consequences of the rigid application of the raising of the school leaving age in respect of our people. I have a boy here now, who if compelled to stay will very probably be destroyed; there is no guarantee as to the success of letting him lead his own life in the 'outside world' but it is the *only* possibility at this juncture. Without the opportunity to take up that chance, hospital or Borstal is inevitable.

65

A parent of a boy who had been playing truant rang my home to tell me how desperate she felt and how she wished something could be done for her son. There are many similar cases which might be solved if the law was made more flexible. Work experience schemes, long supported by teachers of the 'leavers' could provide a breakthrough yet they meet all kinds of obstacles some from the law, some from industry. The National Union of Teachers produced a most progressive document in July 1971 when they were envisaging the changed circumstances following the raising of the school leaving age. In the paper *Work Experience and Secondary Schools* they state:

Work experience should be designed as part of the school curriculum. It should have a two-fold objective, as have many aspects of secondary education: personal enrichment and vocational or further educational relevance. Well-planned work experience should enable aspects of the school curriculum to become more meaningful and significant to the young person. Work experience is far more than a programme for school leavers. It is, rather, the education of the young adult in the difference between one collective institution — the school — with all the human and material supportive agencies that exist for the benefit of the pupils, and another — the factory or firm — which has its own set of supportive agencies, but where personal development of the people involved (i.e. the workers) may be only a minor objective of the organization. Such experience should give a young adult a new sense of consciousness about his abilities and the interests and knowledge he has acquired in school and the possible application of these talents, interests and knowledge in the outside world.

The Union cannot accept, however, that work experience is only relevant to a certain type of pupil with a certain postschool objective. It is desirable that all pupils should have some form of work experience, even on a very limited basis, and that such experience should be integrated into the fifth year curriculum of the school. In the lower forms, the Union is aware of many programmes of educational visits and would welcome an extension of such visits to factories, commercial institutions, hospitals, transport installations and the like, as part of the social education of the pupils, but this aspect of the school curriculum should be clearly demarcated from that of work experience.

The Union is convinced that the full benefits to the pupils, the schools and society at large can only really be derived if work experience schemes are organized on the basis of work participation, as opposed to work observation as known in the educational visit. The pupils must be sufficiently involved in the scheme to enable them to see the world of adults, the work of industry, commerce and service in a new light. They must be involved sufficiently to understand something of the application of their school-acquired knowledge to the working situation. The experience must have sufficient depth to enable the pupil to be more conscious of himself as a young adult with potential to apply in the outside world the several talents which the school has helped to foster, and as such he will be a more thoughtful, self-reliant and self-confident individual.

The document concludes by pointing out that 'the change of law to allow a major work experience programme to be organized by the schools for pupils under the age of sixteen would create many challenges and could have exciting social and educational implications'. I would welcome the setting up of an experimental sandwich scheme which would allow youngsters to gain industrial experience whilst continuing their education on a part-time basis, with the possibility of returning to full-time education on adequate financial grants later.

The recent Report of the National Commission on the Reform of Secondary Education in the USA goes a good deal further. Its most revolutionary recommendation is that the compulsory school leaving age should be lowered to fourteen and this was supported by eighteen out of the twenty members of the Commission. 'If the high school is not to be a custodial institution,' they say, 'the state must not force adolescents to attend'. But they add:

The reduction of compulsory attendance beyond the age of fourteen must follow, not precede, the change in laws which will provide school-leaving youth real alternatives for employment or an alternative mode of education. This recommendation should in no way be considered a convenient way to 'push out' unwanted youth . . . . The change . . . should not be seen as a way to cut the education budget: at least as much money should be spent on the education of these children out of school as would have been spent had they remained in school.

This is an important point and any change of the law in the UK should not be seen as a possible way of saving money within the education service. Indeed, it may cost more to let our rebels leave early and to return when they are ready, but I believe it would be well worth it. The experience of the Open University is already confirming this belief. I was talking to an Open University tutor quite recently who had, amongst his students, several manual workers who had left school at fourteen. They were 'lapping up' this new opportunity to enjoy education at a higher level now that they were mature men and women. Some freely admitted that they had played truant at school and that they would have been very frustrated had they been compelled to stay after fourteen. I would wish to see more generous financial support given by the State to those who wish to follow such courses at whatever age they elect to take them up.

The ILEA has wisely decided to support the unofficial truancy centres run by voluntary organizations and from April 1974 it proposed to regularize the support given by a materials and equipment grant of £30,000 plus the cost of the teachers' salaries. Will more local authorities follow this lead? We desperately need more flexible approaches to the problem of truancy. There is no one answer. The free school is not for everyone and despite the successes (from the childrens' point of view) of Leeds, Liverpool and London no one would advocate them for every child. It is worth noting the comments of Mr Harvey Hinds, chairman of the ILEA Schools Subcommittee reported in the *Times Educational Supplement* on January 11th 1974:

These schools — and the White Lion Street school is one of them — are establishing a completely alternative form of education. We feel at the present time that we are unable to support them, but I hope that we may nevertheless find a way to cooperate with them.

I believe that we may have something to learn from their methods, of their skills in handling children and in forming relationships with children and of what can be added to our own schools. We must find out about the less formal approaches.

In the end we need to spend more money on education and its supporting services if we are to achieve real success. However, the sweeping Government cuts announced in January 1974 seem to rule this out. Even in happier days when that same Government was proclaiming its White Paper *A Framework for Expansion* many teachers were warning of the danger of economy proposals and, in particular, of the reduction in the number of training places available in colleges and departments of education. When will the staffing ratio be such as to permit the small groups and the individual teaching which will foster the potential in each and every child? Must we for ever compromise our children and our future? The growing truancy problem is just one symptom of the society we have created. Are we really surprised that the rebels have a cause?

*Jeremy Seabrook*

# Talking to truants

Trevor, sixteen. Nominally on roll of a London comprehensive; long hair that diminishes his already small face; rather frail preRaphaelite appearance, at odds with the defiant and studiedly aggressive manner. He wears flared jeans, combat jacket, high-heeled shoes that increase his stature, but they are so worn at the heels that they appear very unstable.

'My old lady was educated in a convent, and she thought she was a bit better than my Dad. She thought she was a bit better than everybody. My Dad never worked much. He drunk a lot and he was nasty. I don't blame him; she was always going on about how he showed her up. I went in care a few times, when they separated. I lived down Kent for about six months once. They say I'm maladjusted. They're the ones that are maladjusted. (JS: What, your Mum and Dad? Trevor: No, everybody else.) Anyway, you'd be maladjusted. I've thought about it. What is there not to be maladjusted about? It's like animals in a zoo. You're this, he's that. It makes you like it. If somebody tells you you're maladjusted, you'll get maladjusted. Anyway, like I was saying, if being adjusted means being like everybody else, no thanks. I've got a bad temper, that's all it is really. I stabbed some kid with a pen. Didn't hurt him really. It was nothing. I said, "Next time it'll be a fucking switchblade." I got suspended from school. They took him to a doctor, said it was serious. They had to put a couple of stitches in him; they should've put stitches in his fucking mouth. . . . He was always taking the piss, and I don't like that. I've got this temper. If I think anybody's trying to take the piss, I get mad. I haven't got a temper like I did have. It used to take three teachers sometimes, just to hold me down. They were scared of me. . . . They said I'd have to go away. They sent me to child guidance. "Child guidance," I said, "I'm not a child and I don't want to be guided anywhere." They started threatening me, I'd have to be put away. So that's when I started not going to school. I have got some mates. If I say to them "I'm going up London tomorrow, or down Charlton", they'll come with me. People do what I say. I've got power over them. I haven't been to school this term yet. My old lady knows. She says as long as you keep out of trouble, and keep me out of trouble. So she says I've got nerve trouble. They send somebody from the school board, and there's this threat of taking her to court and she goes berserk and starts praying to God. We don't know where my old man is now. I don't care either. I keep thinking I might see him with all the drunks and dossers down Camberwell or up Waterloo. So when the old lady goes to court she says, "I can't control him, I've tried to do my best" — which she has, only it was fucking useless — and they say I'm a right villain and dangerous. Dangerous. I am. I've got this temper, and I might do something violent. I might. Something violent's been done to me. . . . I just have to make sure people are out of my way when I feel like it. . . . I'm all right if I'm left on my own. . . . I stay in the flat sometimes, play records, as long as the old lady's out at work. Anyway, I'm leaving school now, so it don't matter. I want to get a job in a garage. I like cars. I can drive. I do sometimes, only people don't seem to like it.'

Trevor is very conscious of his image and his apparent nonchalance and boastfulness are very transparent; he is extremely vulnerable and appears to relate very badly to his peers. This seems to be one of the most crucial factors in school avoidance: it is really a means of preventing contact with those of one's own age. However 'boring' or uninteresting or irrelevant school may appear to children (or may be in fact), there is always the consolation of peer-group relationships. It is where these break down that the revulsion seems to be strongest.

Open space, east London. Grass beginning to grow in muddy patches, frail globes of white crocus, green daffodil buds. Two girls about fifteen, on a bench, smoking. Tepid sunshine; one of them screws up her face against the warmth. Hair green-gold at the front, muted scarlet lipstick, wax-pale face, chunky earrings.

'My Mum was seventeen when she had me, and her Mum had just had a kid, so I was brought up like if I was my Nan's kid. I always felt it was funny, because it wasn't made a secret. My Mum called her 'Mum', and I called Nan 'Mum', and everybody used to laugh when I done that, and they said "She ain't your Mum, Barbara is." Big joke. How the bleeding hell can you know if nobody tells you? Anyway, that was my first big problem. Working out who's who; they should've wore fucking labels. Then me Mum got married. I must've been about six. He was forty maybe. Derek. He was bald. My Mum had already got Linda by then, so he was taking her on with two kids, both different fathers. I don't know who Linda's old man is. Don't know whether she does. I don't know mine either, except she goes all stupid if I ask, and says he was somebody well-known. I might have a pop star for a father.

I suppose that's why she had to marry somebody like Derek. Everybody knew she was a bit of a slag. . . . No, I don't mean that. She's very nice really. Big joke. The only trouble is, she thinks she's my sister now. She wants me to go out with her. She wears these short skirts. She's all right, she's thirty-something, she's not old, only I don't want to be mixed up with this we-was-sisters routine. It's embarrassing. Anyway, so there we are. There's my Mum and Derek and Linda and Shaun and Jason and Derry. They might belong to Derek or they might not. She still goes out a lot with other blokes, only Derek don't mind. She doesn't ask him if he minds. She does what she wants. Shaun's nine,

Jason's six, and the baby's four. So the flat's always full of kids. It's a fucking mess. She buys things for the kids to keep 'em quiet, only it don't work. Budgie shit and Trill all over the place. Hamsters, cats, dog. I like the dog though. Kids shouldn't have pets, they're cruel to them. Shaun picks the cat up, holds it under his arm and starts telling it it's naughty, punches it in the face and then wonders why it scratches him. Silly bleeder. So, there's my life. If I go home. Which I don't a lot. So what would I want to go to school for? You tell me. I hop away from home and I hop away from school. You just don't want to be there. I haven't got time for it. I don't want to be pushed around. I've got problems big enough thank you. I can't go and tell them about it can I? I've got a nice woman who's head of year. She used to stand me in front of her, and ask me what she could do to help, and I used to start bawling me eyes out, because she sounded all kind. It was just the sound of her voice like, I never heard a fucking word she said. So I just used to cry. It's a long story. I told her life was fucking terrible. She said, "That's a terrible thing for a girl of your age to say." Which it is. I shouldn't have to say life is terrible. I should be out enjoying meself. I do. I do enjoy meself. I come up here sometimes. It's all right when it's not raining. I do go to school. Some-times. I like cookery. They've got a kitchen and a house, a flat. Bit different from the one I live in. Only thing I ever made was jam tarts. I took some home, Barbara said they're fucking terrible. I meet my mates up here sometimes. There's some boys come up here. I'm not saying what school they go to. (JS: I won't say anything) No. They come up here. I go to their house sometimes at night. His Dad works at Ford's, he's on nights sometimes. I lived with her for a little while. (She indicates her companion, who has remained completely silent throughout.) I told her Mum that I couldn't go home, 'cause Derek fancies me, and I was a bit scared what he might do. Then she got fed up of it, said I was a lazy bitch and turned me out. . . . Eh? No, I don't care if he does fancy me, he wouldn't get far. I'd knock him senseless if he set even one finger on me. If he sets an eye on me even. I can manage him.

I think school is boring. It is boring. I don't know why. I want to have a good time. I do have a good time. Not always, but sometimes. Everybody knows school is terrible, only I'm the only one who stays away. . . . When I go in they all look at you, and teachers say "We've got a special visitor." Big joke. They all turn on you with their eyes, they've all got the dead needle 'cause they daren't do it. Not that I care about that. I'd rather be at school. If it wasn't boring. . . . I don't know, that's their job, not mine. I don't know what isn't boring. . . . Yeah, I know it's boring here, but it's a fucking sight better than school. I can get up and walk away if I want to. Like now. . . .'

Paul, fifteen. For two years Paul has attended his midland comprehensive school unwillingly, and intermittently. He is not so much a school refuser (hypocritical euphemism) as refused by the school; refused, that is, as he really is, as opposed to the conception his teachers and parents have of him. He is a large boy, less adolescent than overgrown child. His parents are very concerned about his lack of progress at school. They themselves are ambitious working class, and have effaced themselves so that their children should be able to get on. Paul has a brother in the academic stream of the same school, and a sister at teacher training college.

For years he has been told that he has it in him, that he doesn't try, that he makes no effort, that he has an intelligence that he won't use. This assessment by the school conforms with his parents' own interpretation. His mother has been a regular visitor at the school, and a kind of conspiracy has evolved between home and school to push him. On the one hand, his teachers have always been very impressed by his mother: 'He's got a lovely home', 'She really does try', 'If all our parents were like that we'd have no problems'; while Paul's mother and father cannot bear to admit that one of their children is conspicuously less well-endowed than the others. His father is inclined to say, 'He's lazy, he doesn't want to learn, he needs a rocket up his backside.' The reality seems to be that Paul is less clever than his brother and sister, and that he is just bright enough to be acutely conscious of this. He has always been compared unfavourably with them. He overcompensates by getting into trouble at school;

'Wherever there's trouble, you won't find Paul far away,' is a weary resigned staff response.

'Do you know what I'd be happy doing? I'd like to be a cook. I like cooking. I like food. Perhaps I'm just greedy. . . . But if I say I want to be a cook, at home they'd go mad. I've always been compared with Graham and Pauline; they're all right about it, only the teachers and Mum and Dad don't know what they do to me. I hated Graham for a hell of a time, I used to have the idea of murdering him. . . . I got into trouble a lot at school. I used to dread going in if we'd got English because I couldn't do it; my mind went blank when he said "Write something"; and so I started playing up. . . . My Dad says, "I used to play up when I was at school, and I wish to God I hadn't." He thinks if he hadn't played up he might've been something good, better then he is now. He works for a builder. He says he might've had his own business if he hadn't mucked about at school. But I used to muck about because that way I didn't have to do the work . . . not because I'm lazy. It used to scare me. So I got ill, and said I had the bellyache or toothache, and I got my Mum to write notes on days we had English. . . . But in the end she stopped, because she knew I was foxing. Which I was. I can read all right, well, I can read enough. . . . They say, "How will you go on when you have to fill in forms, how will you go on when you have to do all these things?" And I say, "Graham can do it." It don't matter to me. . . . (JS: What sort of trouble did you get into at school?) I used to break things, I hid things so when the teacher came in, he couldn't find any chalk, couldn't find a duster. I lost books. . . . You could get so it took so much time getting started that the lesson was finished. . . . Mondays we used to have a double period in the morning. That was terrible. We used to read round the class. . . . Do you know what I used to do? I knew there was a lot of words I didn't know, so I used to stop at things that everybody knows, like "and" and "if" and "but", and all the kids used to laugh, and he got mad. . . . I spent most the lessons standing outside the headmaster's room; that's where they used to send anybody they couldn't control. Then when the head-master came out he'd see you and take you in his study and then give you a punishment. I got sticked a few times. Didn't mind that. (JS: What was it that scared you though; you said you used to be scared of going to school?) It was when I couldn't do the work. They might laugh. . . . So I never let them get a chance. (JS: You made them laugh deliberately, so they shouldn't find out you couldn't cope?) Yeah. You know, I'm not backward like. I mean, we have had kids that were backward, only they couldn't read at all. . . . Sometimes my Dad calls me dibby; Graham used to take the mick, only he doesn't now. . . . They used to make Pauline sit down with a book and say "You teach him", and she did, only I didn't want to know. . . . You don't want your sister teaching you, not when you've been at school all day. . . . When I wag it, I go on my own. I have been with mates a few times, but I go on my own. I used to pinch money out me Mum's bag and go to the pictures. I used to get on a bus. . . . I went down the allotments, in the shed there when it was raining. . . . I went round the shops. I nicked things, only not much, pencils and sweets and fags. You can't nick fags very easily because they always put them out of reach. All the shops have got glass in front of the sweets, so I ask for a quarter of something off the top shelf, then when they've turned round you can reach over and help yourself. Near the school, there was a shop with an old boy who was half blind, and once I got a jar of sweets. A big one. He never found out. . . . I didn't like not going to school. I went round the cake shops, looking at the things in the windows, because that's what I'd like to do. In fact, they asked me at school what I wanted to do, and they said I might get a job in a confectionery firm. But only if I go to school. I don't mind so much now, because I'm going to leave soon. But when I was a bit younger, it was horrible.'

Terry left school three years ago. I met him in connection with a book I am preparing on homosexuality; he talked at some length about his school, and the way in which he became separated from his peer-group. This gave him an extraordinary sense of detachment from school, and a feeling of contempt for what he regarded as an irrelevant prolongation of childhood. In spite of the ostensible democratization of the school, its liberal atmosphere, the sympathy and goodwill of its staff, nothing really reached him; and his precocious sexuality caused him to be absent for long periods of time.

'Well I used to despise school. I thought it was childish. I think the reason was that I got initiated into sex very early on. I was only twelve when I had my first experience. I wasn't seduced or anything traumatic, I mean, I knew what I wanted, and I think I'd known since I was about eight or nine. I went with this man — well, he was eighteen, only to me he was an adult — and we used to go to the pictures and swimming, and he used to take me to eat in Wimpy bars. I thought it was fantastic. I went to his flat sometimes. He didn't rape me or do anything that scared me. If anything, I made the first moves. That lasted till I was about fifteen, and then he gradually dropped me, but by that time I didn't mind, because I knew my way around by then. He had older gay friends who I thought were very sophisticated, and I used to go out with them to pubs. I know it sounds incredible, but I looked much older than I was, and whenever I was asked how old I was I used to say nineteen. You never have to say eighteen, otherwise they get suspicious. . . . So when I went to school and I saw all the kids of my own age sniggering over some dirty pics, I used to feel all superior, because I'd actually experienced all the things they were having fantasies about. . . . It meant that I was always with older people; in a way that made me mature. I got so that I used to come up to London at weekends. Once, I even picked somebody up in Piccadilly Circus, because I thought I'd like to make some money, but as I hadn't got anywhere to go, and he was a foreigner, it never came to anything. . . . I left school when I was sixteen, just before the O levels. I was supposed to be very bright, I don't know. I regret it in a way now. I thought that I was finding out all about life. I was. But I neglected a lot of other things. My parents weren't really interested in me. There were four of us, and all they were concerned about was when I was going to start earning some money. They never queried anything about where I went. My father worked for the local council, only labouring. We lived in a council house. I was very ashamed of them. I decided I wanted some-thing better. I don't know that I've succeeded. .... I suppose I had problems really. There was nobody at school I could've talked to about things like that. They'd would have gone mad, or sent for the police. But you know I had my needs, and I went out and got them satisfied the only way I knew. And that was chance. I only met Jim through going up the park, and sitting around not far from the toilets. I was lucky. I might've met somebody who would've raped me or, I don't know, anything. .... I went from being a child to being grown up. School bored me silly. I used to feel superior to the other kids and to the teachers as well, because they talked to us as if we were children. I was playing games at school, and I wanted to be myself. Why shouldn't I be myself, if that's what I was?'

It seems to be far more likely that persistent adolescent truants have problems with peer-group relationships rather than the school being at fault (except insofar as schools, for all their counselling, social work and welfare orientation, find it virtually impossible to break into the secret world of adolescents and their relationships with each other.) In any case, schools always exaggerate their importance in the socializing process. They come at least fourth in the order of influence in most children's lives, well behind that of contemporaries, parents and the all-pervasive values of the culture which are absorbed unconsciously from the prevailing morality, attitudes, beliefs. The school can be a sort of benevolent foster-parent (a conception beloved by teachers) in the lives of exceptional children, especially clever ones from working-class or disturbed backgrounds; but in most cases, it is merely concerned with the fine tuning of a process which is dictated by agencies that have nothing to do with the elaborate rituals of education.

*Jack Kahn*

# School phobia or school refusal?

School attendance has been compulsory in Great Britain for
three generations. Education is, in the main, a matter of willing and often enthusiastic cooperation of three parties —
parent, child and school. Nevertheless, universal elementary
education had to be presented in the first place to large
sections of the population who did not value its aims and
who were only too conscious of the loss of services or
earnings of their young children. The compulsory element
remains as an essential factor in the consideration of absence
from school, unless there is a 'satisfactory' explanation, such
as illness or the provision of adequate education at some
place other than school.

We are still, however, only too familiar with the incidence
of children kept away from school for the parents' con-
venience. There is the girl whose age has scarcely reached
double figures, but who has reached a stage of domesticity
that is invaluable to the inadequate and harassed mother of
many still younger children; and the boy who assists parents
or acquaintances in enterprises in which they are self-
employed — occasionally of doubtful legality. There are
other cases where absence from school is a positive choice of
girls or boys making their own explorations of the world
around them. Some of them may be taking an active part in
the modern youth culture. Thus, there are not only those
who find interest and satisfactions in woods and fields,
dockyards and railway stations, there are also those who
gravitate to the discotheques, pop groups and communes.

There are also many 'problem families' where failure of a child to attend school is merely one of many failures to conform to accepted rules of society.

There is another type of failure of school attendance where the child says he is *unable* to go to school, and this school refusal has been described as 'school phobia'. It differs both from truancy without the knowledge of the parent and from withdrawal of the child from school by the parent. The parents and the child aver their wish for school attendance. The social conditions may be those of the respectable and respected citizen. The child's school performance may have been satisfactory, and his intelligence could be at any level from the subnormal to something in the highest ranges. In the first cases to come to notice, it was the high level of intelligence of the child, and the high social aspirations of the parents, which helped to distinguish the problem from the stereotype of prolonged truancy. It was recognized there was no physical illness and often no problem had been reported in the child's previous behaviour at home or at school.

There is some significance, too, in the fact that these cases become channelled through the family doctor to consultant pediatricians or psychiatrists. The staff of child guidance clinics did not seek out these children by means of any study of truancy. The cases were initially selected by others, and brought to them by parents, teachers, or family doctors who were aware of some anomaly in the initial formulation of the reasons why the child was not attending school. Once this condition was given shape and a name, it became possible to identify the same problem in children of low levels of intelligence, and in families from all social strata including those where, at one time, the bad general social conditions might have concealed the emotional problems of the individual members of the family.

The very fact that the result of the condition is that the child fails to attend school places it in line with the condition of truancy, with which people are more familiar, and where absence from school is voluntary. Truancy is a *social* problem which, nevertheless, has consequences for the personality development of the individual concerned.

School phobia is a *clinical* problem but it has social implications. When absence from school is a symptom of disturbance, it cannot be kept secret within the family in the same way as night fears, bed-wetting, or food fads. Society as a whole has a share in the problem; not only are parents sensitive to the problem being brought into the open: a law is seen to be violated, yet initial counter measures may fail. Further, teachers feel that a child's truancy, or equally his fear of school, is a reflection on them; and social workers in social service and education departments may feel they have failed when they, too, cannot succeed in getting a child to return to school. School phobia is a psychosocial disorder (Kahn 1968). It came into existence as a psychiatric disorder, but the social component can never be ignored. It is a symptom expressed in behaviour which is a problem to parents and to teachers and, seeing that the result is that the child escapes an obligation imposed by the community, it is also an affront to society. It is distressing to the child too.

Everyone is disturbed by the fact that the child seems to be getting away with something. What is going to happen to a child if he does not go to school? What about his future career? Will he be a normal adult? How can the education welfare officer enforce attendance on those who really truant if it is possible to get away with nonattendance by calling it 'school phobia'? The symptom thus becomes a challenge to the teacher, the education authorities, the parents, the medical profession and to society as a whole.

As a clinical concept, a fairly well agreed pattern of symptomatology became established. Tables of contrasting points were drawn up to help to distinguish school phobia from truancy (Hersov 1960). There is rather less agreement about aetiology, psychopathology, and about the indications for treatment.

The process of separating some phenomenon of human experience and identifying it by investigation which leads to a diagnosis follows a tradition which has become accepted in medical practice. The next steps should be the ascertainment of incidence and prevalence rates, and comparison of the results of different types of treatment (or of no treatment). Many attempts have been made to do this with school phobia without taking into account the fact that the behaviour which leads the psychiatrist to the diagnosis may not be acknowledged as a psychiatric problem by professional workers who come into contact with the child before the psychiatrist can do so. The identified cases represent an unknown proportion of a larger number of cases where the same kind of behaviour and experience either escapes formal recognition or is dealt with, when noticed, on the basis of some other kind of explanation.

Factors held responsible for the symptom (Nursten 1958) include the following:

1 *At school* Bullying, sexually disturbing incidents with other children, a fear of undressing for PT, fear of some particular teacher representing some aspect of school discipline. The peak age is eleven years, and it is then associated with transfer from the primary school to a secondary school.
2 *At home* Parental illness, change of financial and social circumstances, moving from another district, the birth of siblings, or incidents connected with siblings.

Many parents justify the absence of the child from school by fitting the symptoms into the pattern of physical illness (Kahn 1968). The doctor examines the child, and reassures the child and parents, saying there is nothing physically wrong, but appears to accept the physical framework. He gives the child 'nerve tablets', and suggests a return to school in two or three days. The child may get there, sometimes accompanied by the parent to the gate or even into the classroom, but he may return home in the middle of the morning or at midday break. He fails to resume attendance the next day. This is sometimes followed by physical investigations, hospital admission, and even a spell in a convalescent home. On the child's return home, the difficulty with school attendance persists, and by this time the child and his family are terrified that something very obscure is amiss.

New dimensions of understanding of the problem came in stages. Broadwin recognized unusual features of truancy in 1932. Partridge (1939) described psychoneurotic groupings in his new classification of truancy. Adelaide Johnson (1941) was the first to use the phrase 'school phobia', and her most impressive study of the dynamic personal and interpersonal processes in mother and child laid the foundation of the psychotherapeutic approach to the problem. This was as important an advance in the identification and treatment of disorders in the school child as the recent invention of the phrase 'battered baby syndrome'. Now that we have a name for the condition we can recognize it. Similarly, the use of the term 'school phobia' has served to alert the family doctor, the teacher, and members of the public, to the emotional factors in absence from school.

Warren (1948) gave a clear description of the family involvement in school phobia. He referred to 'a neurotic illness which may involve the whole family circle'. Fathers, nevertheless, continued for some time to be thought of as difficult to bring into treatment, and emphasis was often placed on the interaction with the mother alone. Some writers have described school phobia as merely a representation of separation anxiety, and to them the term 'school phobia' would seem unnecessary. Others again have called attention to failure to be able to attend school in children and adolescents with depression and psychoneurotic conditions, linking the symptom with disorders in the mental life of the individual child.

The name 'school phobia' seems inescapable, although many workers including Jean Nursten and myself (1968), have preferred the term 'school refusal' in order to give recognition of wider ranges of pathology, to point comparisons with other disturbances at an earlier stage of life (such as food refusal), and in order to make it possible to refer to wider cultural and community involvement. Thus, in brief, 'school phobia' is likely to be seen as a diagnosis of an individual disorder; 'school refusal' is a complex psychosocial phenomenon.

The following brief descriptions of four cases are quoted as illustrations of points arising from the treatment.

*Case 1*
Boy aged eleven; IQ 128. Born when his mother was forty-five years of age. One brother, thirteen years older, had a successful academic career and had married near the time of his graduation. The patient's symptoms began at about this time. He had been unable to attend school for three months before the first interview. He had been taken on occasions by the father as far as the school ground, but would not enter. Force had been threatened but not used. Attempts caused attacks of panic associated with dizziness and feelings of

unreality. The anxieties were explained by the patient in terms of fears regarding his parents — fears that they might die or separate.

In his earlier childhood he had been quiet, easily controlled, and never naughty. This school attendance difficulty was thought of in terms of disobedience, but hysterical attacks and the disturbances of feeling made attempts at coercion impossible. He had retreated to bed during the fortnight before the first interview and demanded that his father should sleep with him. Treatment was carried out by domiciliary visits at weekly intervals for nine months and then continued for a further six months at a child guidance clinic. Attendance at an independent grammar school was established. He had lost eighteen months of school life, and on entering his new school he was a year older than his classmates.

*Case 2*
Girl aged eleven. Seen for first time six months after break in school attendances. Father a refugee of superior intelligence; the patient was the child of a second marriage to a middle class English woman sixteen years younger than the father.

School absence began at the time of entry into a secondary grammar school. She had previously attended a small private school and had obtained a grammar school place in the secondary selection examination. At the time that absence began, there was trouble at home because of her untruthfulness about losing or mislaying clothing and articles bought when shopping for mother. An attempt had been made to deal with school refusal by transfer to another grammar school and then return to the old school, but both failed. Panic states occurred when she was taken to school and she always returned home shortly afterwards.

IQ 152 plus. Rorschach test showed psychotic features. She maintained progress in school work parallel with her age group by study voluntarily carried out at home. She was treated for one year, but school attendance was still not established, and she was then admitted into a psychiatric in-patient unit for adolescents. On her discharge, six months later, she remained at home and received visits from a home teacher.

*Case 3*

Boy aged twelve. Father a clerical officer who had died three years previously of a coronary thrombosis. Mother now works part-time in father's old post, and is at home at beginning and end of school day. IQ 139 but failed to get grammar school place. One older sibling – sister aged thirteen – attending a grammar school.

School attendance had failed for only a few weeks before referral. Refusal explained by the boy as due to fear that something might happen to his mother during his absence. On occasions during the previous term he had returned home during the lunchbreak to 'phone his mother at work'. This boy helps his mother with the housework more than his sister does, but also torments the mother by bouts of temper, storming at her. He sleeps badly, and reads books and practises his scout knots in the middle of the night to tire himself. Prefers girls' school stories. Often goes to mother's bedroom to complain about sleeplessness. Perfectly behaved when absence from school is accepted. School attendance reestablished within one month of starting treatment; treatment continued.

*Case 4*

Boy aged eleven; IQ 138. Only child. Refusal to attend school began at the start of a new term after absence from school due to chicken pox and influenza near to the end of the previous tern. There had been a removal to another district three months before the onset of the symptoms. When asked to go to school he kicks, screams, shouts, and swears at his parents, and throws articles about. The attacks cease if no attempt is made to send him to school. A domiciliary visit was paid at the request of the family doctor who had been called in because the boy had barricaded himself in his bedroom and was stated to be damaging his furniture.

The father is a semiskilled operative and the only one of his family who did not have a grammar school education. He has brothers in posts of professional status. It would appear that this boy has a higher intelligence than either parent. Both mother and father state that the boy's behaviour would not have been tolerated in their childhood. The father said that in his place he would have been flogged and put on bread and water. They expect instant obedience from the boy, but lately he has been rebellious and would not apologise for what was described as rudeness to relatives. It was stated that on two occasions the boy had run out of the house after a scene, and the father had gone to the police in the erroneous belief that he had run away from home. The help of the probation officer had also been sought. In this case it was decided to send the boy to an 'open-air' school for three months and to arrange psychotherapy in the child guidance clinic on his return.

These cases have been selected for features which help to make the symptoms of school refusal intelligible. The child defeats all attempts to coerce attendance; he is distressed when the attempt is being made, and perfectly normal when his absence from school is accepted. The distress is very real. To understand the symptom it is necessary to make the assumption that the results of the symptom are partly desired (it should also be recognized that there is a parallel wish to have it cured). It is desired by the child or by the parent, or by both. The symptom represents a disorder of child-parent relationship, with particular reference to the imminence or onset of adolescence. There is some degree of conflict in every home at the time of a child's adolescence. School refusal is an intense expression, and illustrates three aspects of the conflict.

First, there are conflicts within the parents. Every parent wishes partly to keep the child as a baby. There is love for the childishness of the young child and fear of the restlessness of the adolescent, who is growing away from his parents' control and sharing strange interests with strange people. Case 1 followed what was virtually the loss of a treasured older son through educational success and an unexpected marriage. The boy showed some perception of this by recounting a dream in which the picture of a wedding was confused with a funeral. In another case, not quoted above, a mother promised to see that her daughter of twelve would attend school, even if she had 'to take her there in a pram'.

Second, there are conflicts within the child. The urges towards independence in a child are often accompanied by fears of inadequacy. A child has the need to be dependent as much as to seek independence. Adolescence is a disturbing phase and, at the onset, children seek the privilege of alternating between the demand for the rights of the grown-up and the desire for the comforts of infancy. At any stage of life an individual is inclined to regress in the face of crisis. This regression can be the main symptom of a serious disturbance and at its greatest severity it can be associated with psychotic symptoms. The temper tantrum, normal to a child of three, can be frightening to the parents when occurring in a child with the physical strength of his (say) twelve years chronological age. It is equally frightening to the child; the growing physical strength and beginning of sexual maturity are both very disturbing (as in cases 2 and 3). Regression is felt to be safer than growing up.

Third, there is the conflict between parent and child. Some parents are reluctant to relinquish the authority which they hold over the child in his earlier years, although the nature of the authority demanded may seem inappropriate to the child's new status. This reluctance is most frequent where the previous authority had been only precariously held by weak parents. The child's growth in intelligence, physique and sexual maturity is looked upon by such parents as a threat. A young child, approaching the parent's level of intelligence, if not of experience, may begin to challenge the parent on his own ground. School attendance may be just one field where the parents' authority is tested; and of the two contending parties it is the child who is the one most disturbed when he is successful. If the symptom does, in fact, leave the parent helpless, the child too is in a weak position. It is very disturbing for a child of eleven to feel that he is the strongest person in his household. In such a household, the parent feels aggrieved. This father has done nothing wrong, yet feels he has failed. If he has been strict, his own parents were even more strict. He knows of parents who are more strict even today, and their children show them complete respect. On the other hand, he says, some parents neglect their children, and yet they seem to have no trouble. Sometimes such a parent explains how tolerant he has been, but expects the results of tolerance to give the complete subservience that the rigid authoritarianism of a previous generation was understood to have obtained.

Such parents complain of the changing patterns of society, and they have justification. The weak tyrant, who wants the results that strength might have given, finds no support in the prevailing culture. He seeks to reinforce his authority by taking his child to the probation officer, or to a policeman, 'to give him a fright', and finds that his child has been brought up to look upon the policeman as a friend and is not afraid of him, and the probation officer neither jumps to the conclusion that the child alone is in the wrong nor provides an immediate remedy.

Rational therapy of any disturbance should be derived from concepts of the process responsible for the disturbance. Conversely it should be possible to infer the way in which failure to attend school is envisaged from the nature of the attempts to deal with it. If, for example, the efforts are entirely restricted to the application of compulsion, it is evident that no importance has been attached to the inner or interpersonal life of the individuals concerned. Within the framework of medicine, treatment ostensibly is directed to a pathological process and prevention is based on aetiology, but at no stage has organized medicine been without reliance on many empirital procedures in methods of treatment which have no basis other than the fact that they are believed to be effective. Moreover, when rationality is abandoned, effectiveness is not always insisted upon. It is sufficient to believe that the treatment is the 'right' treatment. The varieties of treatment for school refusal are an indication either of the different viewpoints on the nature of the disorder believed to be present, or they represent ideas about how children should behave. Compulsion may be in mind even when prescribing for what is thought of as a disorder qualifying for psychiatric or other medically-based treatment. Compulsion is the medical prescription!

Thus treatment ranges from psychotherapy for the individual or the family, to drugs and behaviour therapy. Furthermore, a 'medical' prescription may be given for some educational procedure such as change of class or school, or curriculum! The psychiatrist, the psychologist and social worker working in child guidance clinics may join in the investigation and treatment, sharing in some common philosophy. Alternatively, the individual members of·the team may have divergent viewpoints which they are able to express in different settings outside the clinic. At the same time, other professions are called upon to give their particular contribution. Teachers, education welfare officers and various committees and courts are given responsibilities regarding school attendance. They may wish to apply the label of 'treatment' to the decisions on which someone has to act.

Psychotherapy is the treatment prescribed by those who relate the behaviour to an underlying psychopathology. Simultaneous casework with the parents recognizes their participation in the disturbance and in the therapeutic process. Conjoint family therapy emphasizes the view that family interaction has a normality and a pathology. Some aspects of the thoughts and behaviour of individual members can be looked upon not as their own exclusive property but as part of the family process. These aspects are influenced and change only in the presence of, and with the involvement of, other members of that family. The choice of individual or family treatment should not depend upon an ideological view. It should be possible to identify the nature of the conflict and its main focus, and the choice of treatment can then be made on recognizable criteria.

Drug treatment bypasses the nature of the inner mental processes and interpersonal relationships. It concentrates on the relief of anxiety through pharmacological action on biochemical processes. The justification is that when anxiety (from whatever cause) is no longer operating, some people are able to resume behaviour in accordance with 'normal' expectations. The conflicts are not explored if the problem ceases to exist. Behaviour therapy is based on learning theory which is supported by animal experiments. School refusal is looked upon simply as abnormal behaviour. Normality is either restored (or established for the first time) by gradual introduction to (or enforcement of) normality as represented by school attendance. It differs from parental or legal coercion by the precise nature of instructions of how to get the child to school. Behaviour therapy has the advantage of concentrating on what the child does. It is felt that it is possible to leave aside the question of how the child thinks, feels, and interacts.

Alongside the procedures related to a therapeutic setting, there may be many coincidental or sequential decisions such as removal to a residential school. There may be court hearings which result in a supervision order, or a care order, involving removal of the responsibility for the child from the

89

parent to the social services department of a local authority. A child may be removed to a childrens' home, to a community home, or remand home of approved school type intended to provide a disciplined environment in which school attendance is taken for granted. Occasionally the order is intended to make it possible for a child to receive treatment which the parents refuse. There are still instances where what amounts to removal to an approved school is ordered without considering alternative ways of understanding and treating the underlying problems. On other occasions this may be an agreed decision of the psychiatric and social services department when it is necessary to draw upon the force of law.

Much of what has been written about school refusal implies acceptance of the problem as a personal or inter-personal disturbance of individuals and families. It is mainly a psychiatric concept. The social dimension is added particularly in the case where truancy is a possible alternative label. I have taken the view that in school refusal the social dimension always has some importance, and that in truancy the individual personality factors should be taken into consideration. In both these dimensions, however, it appears that we have excluded any part that is possibly played by the school in the genesis of the disturbance. The teachers understandably are made anxious by the refusal of children to accept the education which they offer. They are some-times reassured by the explanation that it is not what is happening in school that the child is afraid of, but what might conceivably happen at home when he is away. Going beyond the school, responsible authorities are concerned that anyone should refuse what is provided for the good of its younger generation. This should carry us to the consideration of the philosophy of education and to the content of school life in any particular school. It ought to be possible to study the question of conflict of children with the school, or the family with the school.

We have been able to evade this dimension of the problem so long as education had some voluntary component. When the school leaving age was eleven, twelve or thirteen years it was only a minority of volunteers who continued education into the teenage years. For these pupils, the school could create a framework of its own choice, which worked satisfactorily enough for those who could fit in. A school is able to justify its curriculum when those who do not adjust exclude themselves, or are excluded. The lengthening of school life for children of all social classes and all levels of intelligence has created new problems which challenge existing educational practice.

The stimulus to enter into this educational dimension comes from within the educational system. Many teachers and administrators are concerned about absence from school in the later years of school life, which is reaching such an extent that it appears impossible to carry out full individual investigations in every case. At this level, changes in educational procedures should have educational validation even if undertaken for the benefit of individual pupils. Changes might involve selective use of informal methods of education (deschooling) or combinations of school and occupational experience.

When the alternative to attendance at school is as far reaching as a legal decision to separate the child from the family, there should be ample justification that this is the best possible decision. At present the criteria are subjective and one of the factors might be frustration and anger with failure of routine procedures which had been successful in other cases.

If school attendance is to retain its compulsory element, there still remains the question of the limits to which compulsion can be extended. The means used must be commensurate with the problem for which compulsion is brought to bear. At present the adolescent, who has within himself the power to resist, has no option other than to be ill or delinquent if he does not attend school. The result is that many of those who may wish to opt out of a system which is not of their choice, and which cannot be altered with their participation, are fitted equally inappropriately into either the therapeutic or legalistic setting.

School refusal thus is a topic which takes us into problems of individual personality, family interaction, and relation-ships with the community organizations. It also takes us finally into the ethical problems of the compulsory public provision of services intended for the individual good.

*References*

BROADWIN, I. T. (1932) A contribution to the study of truancy *American Journal of Orthopsychiatry* 2, 253—9

HERSOV, L. A. (1960) Refusal to go to school *Journal of Child Psychology and Psychiatry* 1, 137—45

JOHNSON, A. M. *et al* (1941) School phobia *American Journal of Orthopsychiatry* 11, 702

KAHN, J. H. (1968) School phobia *Acta Paedopsychiatrica* 4—10

KAHN, J. H. and NURSTEN, J. P. (1962) School refusal: a comprehensive view of school phobia and other failures of school attendance *American Journal of Orthopsychiatry* 32, 707—18

KAHN, J. H. and NURSTEN, J. P. (1968) *Unwillingly to School* Oxford: Pergamon Press (second edition)

NURSTEN, J. P. (1958) The background to children with school phobia *Medical Officer* 100, 340

PARTRIDGE, J. M. (1939) Truancy *Journal of Mental Science* 85, 45

WARREN, W. (1948) Acute neurotic breakdown in children with refusal to go to school *Archive of the Diseases of Children* 23, 266

*Frank Coombes*

# Truancy on trial

Truancy is a problem that is used by many social agencies, especially the press and members of parliament, as the whipping post for numerous social ills. But are we sure we know what truancy is all about? For most people it conjures up pictures of absconding adolescents, bent upon avoiding the teacher-set tasks within the closed community of the school. Unfortunately, it is not as simple as that. Truancy is a small constituent of the total school welfare problem and the whole truth is as difficult to find as the numbers who are affected, and sometimes afflicted, by this emotional maladjustment. Experience and research, such as it is, show that the types of truancy and causal factors are almost as many as the children who succumb to it.

First, let us look at the research into the size of the problem. The result of a sample survey, based on average percentage attendance, may well show the amount of time lost in school, but it will shed no light at all on the motivations of the missing pupils. For example, a teacher with thirty children in a class will produce an acceptable percentage attendance of 90 per cent throughout the month. This may well mean that three pupils were absent throughout the period, or six pupils had two weeks off, or every child in the class had every Friday afternoon off. All these permutations would give the magic 90 per cent attendance but no valid information on the number affected by absence.

The Education Welfare Officers National Association sought to examine twelve selected districts and one large county borough. The conclusions tended to show that where a percentage average attendance of 91.6 was produced, *the number of children actually absent* from school with all known reasons was just over 20 per cent. The figure for a large county borough was about 89 percentage average attendance which pointed to 22 per cent of all pupils being affected by absence each week.

Another technique is the 'single day single absence' system. Schools are asked to submit returns of the number of pupils absent on a particular day, together with the number for whom notes excusing attendance have been received. The trouble here is that in many schools a special one-off effort is made to cut down on the numbers missing. As a result absenteeism is artificially reduced.

To say that we do not know the extent of truancy nationwide with accuracy makes it easier for the publicity-conscious factions to exploit what is, in fact, a very sensitive area of social concern among parents and teachers. Early in 1974, a headmaster of a large London comprehensive school publicized his estimate of truancy at about one million pupils per day or 12½ per cent of the total school population. These figures are probably an exaggeration but if they are anywhere near the truth, truancy is costing the nation somewhere in the region of £200,000,000 in wasted resources. The cost to parents and children in unhappy and unfulfilled relationships and adjustment to settled living is by far the more intangible and disturbing feature of the problem.

The job of quantifying truancy as a part of total absenteeism depends entirely on seeking out the true causes of absence. This requires close and confidential links between the home, the community and the school. A work force of such a size and with sufficient time and skill to carry out this task has not yet arrived on the educational scene, and despite the increased attention given to absenteeism in recent years, very little significant change has been made in the support service to schools. The state system contains just over eight million pupils and 348,000 full-time teachers who together cost the nation £2,200,000,000 annually. There are no national statistics of the numbers of education welfare officers supporting the schools, but the latest reliable research puts the number at about 2,500.

The education welfare service, which has its roots in the compulsory clauses of the 1880 Education Act, later reforms including the introduction of care legislation, milk and meals in school, clothing provisions, grants to widen educational opportunity, and changes to the structures of personal social services, had the effect of confirming the social work content of the education welfare officers' responsibilities, but has done little to advance the national conditions for improved staffing and training. This despite the recommendation of the Plowden Report in 1967 and the Seebohm Report in 1968, out of which the local authority personal social services were forged, leaving the school social work department-alized and separate from other social services. Its slow development and neglected training and staffing is set out in the Working Party Report of the Local Government Training Board — the Ralphs Report — published in April 1973.

But what of the responsibilities of parents? Should not they be supporting the efforts of the welfare officers? The law places upon the parents the duty of ensuring education for every child of compulsory school age. The 1944 Education Act (section 36) states very clearly that 'it shall be the duty of the parent of every child of compulsory school age to cause him to receive efficient full-time education, suitable to his age, ability and aptitude, either by regular attendance at school, or otherwise'. The parent does not necessarily have to send the child to school, provided that the education is full-time, efficient and suitable. Having applied for a child's admission to a school, whether private or state, then regular attendance can be expected and enforced. The lack of definition as to the meaning of 'regular' and 'full-time' can often cause difficulty, but in the main a child must attend from the time set apart for registration and through-out the sessions laid down by the school in its curriculum unless prevented from doing so by illness or other unavoid-able cause. Leave may be given to a child by a headmaster for certain defined reasons but not to avoid tuition, or to become employed, unless that employment is part of an officially recognized work experience scheme under the work experience legislation.

A major problem is deciding what exactly we mean by regular attendance. For example, one local education authority may well instruct its school and education welfare staffs that registration regulations must be strictly observed, while other local authorities allow considerable latitude. Truancy is often affected by the way in which internal school

95

regimes impinge upon the pupils. Lateness is often a source of anxiety to many pupils, and they will avoid entry after the bell has gone, and stay free until a normal entry can be made at the next session. Even if they arrive soon after registration and are marked late, this can be regarded as evidence of irregular attendance for which parents are answerable in law.

Nor can parents claim ignorance as an excuse. In Crump v Gilmore (reported in *The Times* November 4th, 1969) a fourteen year old girl had been absent on twelve occasions out of 114 possible attendances, but her parents were not aware of it. After the magistrates had dismissed the case the Queen's Bench Divisional Court directed them to convict. The parents' ignorance of the absence was irrelevant in law, although a mitigating factor in the final sentence, which was an absolute discharge. Even if the law provides a deterrent for some families who might otherwise encourage their children to avoid school, overall the use of legal processes does little to tackle the underlying anxieties, stresses and strains upon schoolchildren. But this is not to say that the daily session of registration is unimportant. Indeed, for many youngsters it is the most crucial part of their school life. Handled properly it can be a valuable exercise in home/school communication. The child is able to relay to the teacher attitudes, fears, anxieties, all of which may be important to his emotional, physical and mental health. This session is the barometer of the child's total educational difficulties, dilemmas and doubts. It is important that the contract between the headmaster and the parent is constantly kept in mind, for information which inevitably crops up, often unsolicited and unexpected, belongs to the parent in the first instance. The rule of *loco parentis* assumes that the teacher, through the headmaster and other educational staff, will act in the same way as a wise and reasonable parent. It is in the registration session that social work by teaching staff can begin. The communication, or lack of it, with children is a significant factor in detecting those who may be victim to the sort of stresses that lead to absences from school and detract from normal educational development.

I have assessed the probable ratio of absenteeism as one in five children. It is by no means a good measure if we are to bring the problem down to personal and individual proportions. So much depends, as I have already reiterated, upon the school regime, the degree of interest and attitudes of the teaching staff. Another factor is the type of school, whether infant, primary, first school, middle school, grammar, secondary modern or comprehensive. The kind of environment in which the school is set, and the culture or traditional community behaviour will have some bearing upon the responses of the parent toward the school's demands, and the attitude of the child toward 'authority' and the tutors within the school. With no specialized research available to the fieldworker, all these factors are either taken for granted or forgotten. Even professionally-trained teachers and social workers need constant reminding of personal and community social work requirements. The parents, all too often, are expected to remove the causes of truancy but without much in the way of professional advice or help. Yet teachers are eager to accept the credit when children are socially and academically successful.

The lesson we must learn is that the truancy trap exists for all pupils irrespective of their social grouping or individual abilities. Consider some of the victims.

Adele was eight years of age, well clothed and cared for. She would talk freely to her teacher but she had few friends. This extrovert, talkative and rather boastful child arrived at school one morning having been intercepted at 8.30 by her mother as she was leaving home unbreakfasted, and complete with suitcase packed with her personal belongings, and a one pound note, taken the night before from her mother's handbag. Tempers flared and mother's scolding did little more than deepen this antihome feeling and irrational hate of her mother's protectiveness, but minus her case and one pound note she was sent to her junior school in time for registration and morning class. Once inside the school a new plan of action formed in her mind. Taking her one close friend into her confidence, the couple walked out of the school gate at lunch time. Less than half an hour elapsed before the word was passed to the school welfare officer, and within the hour the news that her eight year old daughter had carried out her threat to run away from home was communicated to the mother.

Adele's absence from class in the afternoon was merely another statistic. According to the record, she was absent from school without the knowledge or consent of her mother. But no word of the intense struggle for control in the home by her mother, or of the child's threat to run away, had been passed to the school: the incident of the packed case and the stolen pound note only came to the notice of the teachers after the enquiry had started, and the welfare officer had investigated the absence. The effect upon the parents of the school-friend with whom she had disappeared was electric and alarming, for it turned out that she too had threatened to abscond from home. The return of both children within a couple of hours was greeted by both sets of parents with threats of punishment. More appropriate would have been a total reassessment of the needs of the entire family unit. Truancy from school was in fact truancy from home.

Unfortunately it is becoming all too fashionable to transfer the centre of home difficulty from home to school which, in effect, is a retreat from reality. I expect to see Adele in difficulty in her secondary education, unless her mother can seek help from the school, the education welfare service or one of several agencies that await the call. Without that call little will be achieved.

Christine was just over fourteen years of age when, one fine spring morning, she set out from home with her sister, three years her senior. She left her home giving the impression that she was going to school. There had been some two years of discord between her and her father who, with fairly typical parental concern, had forbidden her to keep company with a particular youth older than herself. Christine was given to lying and aggressive, disruptive behaviour in school. Both school and parent had asked the education welfare officer to arrange an urgent appointment at the child guidance clinic. Her sister had already made an appearance in court and was the subject of a care order. But she had been permitted to move to London and it was her intention to invite her sister Christine into the same flat where lived two, and sometimes three, youths of about twenty years of age. Nine months passed before Christine returned to school, and almost ten months before she was taken into the care of the local authority as being beyond the control of her parents. Her immoral life in London had continued despite the effort of two police and local authority social service departments. Christine's truancy was rooted in her maladjustment toward her family and friends. She was another truancy from home case. No place of safety or security could be devised for her, even though her actions appeared to many to cry out for such refuge.

When we examine truancy we have to take into account many factors other than school attendance patterns. Very often they are factors which do not respond to counselling in school, or to close casework techniques which were available to Christine's home. It is not my intention here to provide final solutions, but is is necessary to take stock of the frustration and complexity associated with many of our laws which are supposed to help the individual child early enough to avoid the collapse of a happy school and home life. The 1969 Children and Young Persons Act has so far failed to bring to schoolchildren the kind of support which they ought to have, and which most harassed parents pray for at the time of crisis. Concepts of authoritarian discipline and strict codes of practice have been undermined by liberal legislation that requires delicate interpretation by parents, teachers and social workers. The social work approach to the personal needs of families and individuals has been attempted with too few personnel in the field, and all too often a sophisticated superstructure of administration has disguised the lack of field work that should be attempted on behalf of all children.

Precise definitions need to be applied to the absentee problem. Many of the attacks made upon the loosening of home and school disciplines cite the deterioration in school attendance as the result. I cast very serious doubts upon wild allegations suggesting that one million children a day go into limbo and escape from school. But the total school tuition loss may well range between 12½ per cent and 20 per cent per day which affects between one fifth and one eighth of the children in school. The extent to which this is due to absence without consent of school or parent cannot be truthfully measured without patent honesty from pupil and parent. Often the first-time truant is protected by notes to school suggesting other more acceptable reasons for absence. Invariably only two people, the child and its mother, know that truancy has set in.

Patterns of home life and parents at work tend to re-move security and control at home, making absence easier undetected. The number of parents working on shifts, and who may be free on days when schools are in session, has increased casual absence with parental consent. At the other end of the problem scale, one parent families are becoming more numerous. I do not claim that these children attend any worse or better than others, but they are more vulnerable to various conditions of family stress and the creation of lively attitudes to learning is not made any easier.

Another feature, comparatively new to education, is the so-called 'internal truancy' which can occur in the large comprehensive school. This can be detected by internal checks but it may occupy the attention of staff who should be otherwise engaged. The extension of internal truancy to forays into the town and into shops possibly involving delinquent acts has been made easier by the introduction of so much project work and the acceptance of free school periods for older pupils. A constant checking of the class register is the only safe precaution in this kind of situation.

There are, therefore, serious implications for the child, parent, school and society at large in the truancy trap, implications which go beyond the loss of school tuition alone. Unless the departments of school administration and school social work are adequate to the present-day needs, and I have seen very few that are, accurate identification of absences will not be achieved quickly enough to deal with individual problems of social adjustment. Above all, reciprocal cooperation between school and home, so that an exchange of information is easily and readily undertaken on both sides, is imperative.

Changes in the structure of schools, and more recently in the reorganization of local authorities, have followed hard upon the 1971 reshaping of the personal social services of local authorities. The Plowden Report ( CACE (England and Wales 1967) and Seebohm Report ( DES 1968) pointed to a need to provide schools with a social work force able to deal effectively with all kinds of social handicaps and capable of working in close collaboration with other agencies dealing with family problems. But neither the new local authority social services nor the education welfare service has been developed to the point of being able to offer the kind of service that is needed. Little improvement can be expected in the light of economies made by the last Government.

The education welfare service has a history of slow development. It developed from the first compulsory attendance legislation of 1870, but the social and educational changes over the last century have broadened the scope of

100

the duties of education welfare officers. Legislation in health matters and social care, milk and meals in school, provision of clothing, grants to aid educational opportunities, the setting up of child guidance clinics and the accent on prevention of breakdown of education, rather than authoritarian approaches, has confirmed the welfare content of their work, and has led to the recognition of their social work role.

One hopeful development is an attempt by the Local Government Training Board to identify the areas of need within the education welfare service. Sir Lincoln Ralphs headed a working party whose terms of reference were to investigate the functions of education welfare officers in order to identify common elements, and to advise the Board on the most appropriate training for them, including a system of examinations. Now the Local Government Training Board has demanded for education welfare officers the same training as that provided for all other social workers and henceforth education welfare officers will require the certificate of qualification in social work awarded by the Central Council for Education and Training in Social Work.

But this in itself will not provide the correct staffing ratio of pupil to social worker in the community. The availability of education welfare workers, with training sufficient to deal with social casework techniques, varies with each local authority. A ratio of one field worker to 2,000 pupils is considered by one expert to be the ideal balance. Yet in the best areas where social work concepts have been adopted, the ratio can be as low as one to 2,500 pupils and the general rule is for an officer to attempt to cope with anything from 4,000 to 6,000 pupils.

To expect the kind of instant service necessary to protect children from truancy, delinquency and stress situations, both at school and at home, to avoid employment exploitation to the detriment of educational opportunity, and to assist parents and teachers in interpreting social stress signals so that children may attend school physically, emotionally and mentally prepared, is a task which, many claim, ought to pass from education authorities to social service departments. I make no special plea on this controversial matter, except to draw attention to the development of many services within the educational structure: the careers advisory service, the youth and community service, the child guidance clinics, the school psychological service, and the school meals service. The need to forge a comprehensive school social work service out of this fragmented pattern is as important now as the amalgamation of the personal social services outside education was in 1971.

*References*

DES (1968) *Report of the Committee on Local Authority and Allied Personal Social Services* (Seebohm Report) London: HMSO

CENTRAL ADVISORY COUNCIL FOR EDUCATION (England and Wales) (1968) *Children and their Primary Schools* (Plowden Report) London: HMSO

*Anna Sproule*

# Local authority experiment: London

To all outward appearances, Sandra is a perfect teacher — calm, cheerful, totally at ease with herself and the teenage London truants she's working with. They think she's great. But, unbelievably, she's only fifteen and more incredibly still this efficient, articulate and friendly paragon is the school board man's nightmare. The hapless education welfare officer in charge of her gets as good as he gives. She doesn't go for being rooted out at 8.30 in the morning by officials with wristwatches and good intentions — 'insult' she says amiably. And she hasn't been near a classroom in months.

> 'In the third and fourth year I used to have days off here and there. Then in the fifth year I just never went at all — I *refused* to go to lessons. Some girls can go back to sitting at desks again after six weeks holiday, but I couldn't stand it, specially since I had a teacher who was twenty-two, and my boy friend is twenty-one. Ridiculous.'

It is ironic that, a hundred years ago, the virtues Sandra undoubtedly has would have brought her praise rather than official disapproval:

> 'I'd rather work than go to school every day. I don't mind work, I like it. I work in a hairdressers' every weekend. I help my family out. When my mum was ill, all the washing was done, and the housework, and the dinner was on the table.'

She aims to take up a hairdressing apprenticeship when — speed the day — school has no further legal claims on her. In the meantime, and with the best will in the world, she finds formal education irrelevant.

Someone, struck by a flash of genius, has remembered the 'poacher turned gamekeeper' adage, and Sandra is now acting as coffee-maker, one-hand typist, girl Friday and general morale booster to a team of London youth workers and the kids they are hoping to reengage in education. 'I like work,' she repeats: end of story that, if not totally happy from her school's point of view, has at least been marked by an element of good will and compromise.

Seen from many angles, London's schools, pupils and teachers are far removed from the educational experience that is normal in this country. But the Inner London Education Authority's difficulties, truancy included, are essentially those of any big inner city authority, struggling to find antidotes to complex social problems that may have only marginal causative links with education.

Mr W. R. Braide, the ILEA's senior assistant education officer in charge of primary and secondary schools, can think of at least five basic reasons for inner city truancy; and only one has a direct link with the schools he administers:

'I would be prepared to admit that some of the blame may attach to the school where, for a particular child, that school may not appear to be offering what he wants — the things that are relevant to the life he is going to lead. He may be rebelling to some extent against what he is offered at school.'

That's factor one. The other four have their roots in such intractibles as traditional inner city culture ('Parents may have antiauthority attitudes — school, for them, is seen to be just another aspect of institutionalized authority, and therefore they're agin it'); economic necessity ('Girls are being kept home to do the chores, boys help out with dad's market stall'); the natural stresses of adolescence, aggravated by difficult home backgrounds; and the nature of London itself ('There are the opportunities offered by the big inner city of just anonymously disappearing from school and wandering about the streets'). In a small country town, children are only too likely to run into someone who knows them and also knows where they should be. But who spotted Sandra on her out-of-school forays? And who cared?

The diffuse, sprawling enormity of the causes that underlie truancy is only matched by the diffuse, sprawling difficulty involved in measuring the phenomenon. According to an ILEA survey carried out in 1971, something like 6,000 secondary pupils (or 3 per cent of the secondary school population) were away from school on a single day for what the authority calls 'unauthorized or unknown reasons'. It sounds watertight enough; but it is not a complete answer. Leaving aside the cases where an 'unknown' reason might have proved perfectly acceptable (if it could ever have been discovered), there still remain the shadowy, unaccounted-for absences of the 'concealed truants'. A concealed truant is an artist: he turns up at school, is marked present on the register and then disppears.

It is a type of truancy, says Mr Braide, that becomes especially possible in the large modern comprehensive with a flexible timetable: 'We didn't find huge numbers of them in 1971, but we did find evidence that this kind of truancy was taking place.' (A spot check in Tower Hamlets supported this finding. The check, taken at five different times on a variety of test days, showed that an average of twenty-eight pupils absented themselves from school at any one period after having been registered as present.)

If every teacher in every secondary school kept his own class register for every lesson, the extent of concealed truancy in the ILEA would be concealed no longer. But, as the last year has shown, London secondary teachers are hardpressed enough already. In a sense, this is the heart of the dilemma. Truancy is an educational problem; but London teachers, by themselves, cannot hope to solve it totally. The causes are too deep-seated, the effects too difficult to trace, and the treatment too timeconsuming. This is not to say that the ILEA have not urged its employees to make special efforts, as Mr Braide points out:

'We're asking schools to play their part. They are on the look-out for truants. Again, we're taking every possible step to encourage schools to see that their curriculum and methods, especially at the upper end of the school, are applicable to these pupils and attractive to them.'

The education welfare officers, too, have a 'very clear duty in regard to school attendance'.

But the writing on the wall is clear; a complex issue needs a complex answer. Bring in everyone who has something to offer. Cooperate or go bust. This was the thinking of Mr Reg Peirce, divisional education officer for Tower Hamlets and the City of London, and the man behind one of the best-organized preventive drives London has so far taken against truancy. His scheme, which was put into action in the autumn of 1973, was basically simple: to 'coordinate and reinforce' all the services who have contact with truants or potential truants.

Thus, a campaign leaflet explains, parents should tell the school immediately if their child is absent; schools will let parents know when their child is away without good reason, and will make sure that all returning pupils are seen personally by a teacher; education welfare officers will visit the homes of pupils who are absent without just cause; borough social workers will try to persuade regular truants to go back to school; youth workers will keep an eye out for teenagers who turn up at clubs when they should be at school; doctors will excuse children from school attendance only when they are really unfit to go; and the police will be on the look-out for children wandering the streets in school hours. About 400 out of the 11,000 secondary pupils in the division play truant each day. 'We want those 400 back in school – off the streets, out of mischief, in the classroom preparing for a useful career,' say the campaign organizers in their appeal to parents. 'Help us, help your child.'

Mr Peirce deprecates the fact that his task has been made all the more difficult by the notorious London teacher shortages (part-time schooling is an ideal alibi for a suspected truant); he is also cautious about the effects his campaign has had, 'It's an ongoing problem; we'll never get a result in the sense that, "there was once a 3 per cent truancy rate, now it's 1 per cent".' However, a comparison between the figures for absence for unacceptable or unknown reasons in 1971 and a second set drawn up in October 1973 shows that the percentage of 'U & U absenteeism' had gone down from 29 per cent to 17.5 per cent of total absences. At the same time, the total number of pupils truanting from school in October 1973 was no higher than it had been two years earlier.

Mr Peirce carefully points out that there are no comparable figures for 1973 from other London divisions where no special campaigns were attempted. This makes assessment of his own antitruancy drive difficult. But, at least, 'noone has said that things are worse'. These uncertainties are, of course, the lot of anyone who tries his hand at preventive rather than curative techniques. Who can say how many children decided *not* to play truant in the face of such well-concerted opposition? However, the ILEA are now investigating a new type of curative measure that may, with luck and the resources needed for sophisticated followup work, produce more definable results.

At the beginning of 1974 they announced they were expanding their support for 'informal education' — education carried on outside the formal school framework for children who did not accept ordinary schooling. From 1974–5 onwards, the ILEA would be providing part- and full-time teaching help, plus grant aid, for the informal education set-ups in the city: set-ups like the Rainer Centre in south-east London for difficult boys, which already had a grant and two ILEA teachers at its disposal; or Rosemary House, which is a centre established at the Peckham Adventure Playground for pupils not attending one of two local schools. This already had two ILEA teachers on secondment, helping to 'provide a fresh approach and environment for pupils who are persistent nonattenders, with a view to getting them back into their schools.' This idea of 'getting them back' is at the heart of the ILEA's thinking on the matter. 'A period of more or less individual tuition in a more informal atmosphere than a school could well be of real benefit to these children,' said a report accepted by the ILEA's schools subcommittee, pointing out at the same time that it was 'unrealistic' to think this could be done quickly or easily. But, however slow or difficult the operation may prove to be, informal education teams may now apply for ILEA help as long as they concur with the 'get them back' aim, as long as they are willing to work in cooperation with local secondary schools, as long as they have enough cash to lay on suitable premises, and as long as the ILEA have a say in the secondment and work of the teachers involved. ('A distinction must be made,' the report adds somewhat tetchily, 'between the centres described above and the

107

so-called "free schools" . . . although pupils may move back from free schools to maintained schools, this is not what the free schools set out to do.')

The list of establishments that hoped to get ILEA help or already had some when the report was made, shows how much support the 'cooperate or go under' motto commands. The fight against truancy crosses all departmental boundaries. Lyndhurst Hall, for example, is a day-care centre, taking up to eight children who are not going to school. It was established and is run by the social services department of the London Borough of Camden, and has an ILEA teacher on the staff. There are the transitional classes at the John Scott and Shoreditch health centres in Hackney; with a teacher in charge of each, they together cater for up to twenty school refusers, but are under the overall supervision of the health centres' child guidance clinics. There is the Cromartie Road Annexe, which acts as a centre for pupils who are truanting from either Archway or Tollington Park School in north London.

The Annexe, an enterprise run jointly by the ILEA and the Islington Family Service Unit, is staffed by two teachers and a social worker. Numbers of pupils vary, but are usually somewhere around the twelve to fifteen mark. When one of them is eventually ready to return to school, he can choose which of the two schools he wants to return to: if he wants to go back with his mates, that's all right; if he prefers to make a fresh start, that's all right, too. Furthermore, he is accompanied on his return by one of the Annexe staff, who smooths his introduction, eases out any difficulties with his teachers, and metaphorically holds his hand.

The Adelaide Centre in Camden, which is run by the borough's social services department, works in conjunction with the Kingsway College for Further Education in Bloomsbury. The Adelaide Centre is different in that it does not deal with truants as such. Its aim is to help emotionally disturbed youngsters in their symptoms of disturbance. 'It's difficult to know whether they are truanting because they are disturbed, or whether being away from school adds to their emotional problems,' says Mr Michael Bees, head of Kingsway's social and community studies department, which handles the Kingsway end of the operation. (It has provided an educational programme for the Adelaide's students to follow, along with teachers; and it also tries to get the students placed in jobs.)

The Adelaide's staff bridge departmental boundaries in fine style. There are three social workers, the full-time academic tutor from Kingsway, two part-timers who specialize in arts and crafts and woodwork respectively, a consultant psychiatrist who comes in for two sessions a week with the staff, and a liaison social worker from the borough itself. There is also a cook/housekeeper who is experienced in working with maladjusted children, and telephone-answering is liable to be done by the students themselves.

Mr Michael Lally, the Adelaide's organizer, describes the teenagers he works with as 'fairly confused' — either withdrawn or very aggressive:

'They are children who could not be tolerated in school: they would either be excluded or else exclude themselves by not going. The vast majority have had nine months away from school before they come to us.'

The day's business starts at 9.30 and goes on until four in the afternoon. Sixteen full-time students are usually in attendance (the attendance rate, says Mr Lally, is 'phenomenal'), with another eight who come in for counselling twice a week. The first session of the morning is spent in group work — possibly academic, possibly not, such as rehearsing a rock musical. Then lunch, which forms an integral part of the Adelaide's therapeutic activities. Deciding what to eat is a communal affair; so is helping to cook it and cleaning up afterwards. After an hour's break, it's back to work. 'We consider anything that's a contribution to the well-being of the centre or the individual as a work situation.'

Mr Bees sums up:
'What they are getting is a great deal of personal support from the workers there. They are allowed to work out their feelings and aggressions, and these are dealt with in the group they are in whereas in school you have to repress these.'

One index of the Adelaide's success is the number of students it feeds through to the college itself. 'Out of the sixteen there, about twelve now attend the college for about twelve hours a week.'

In addition to its Adelaide work, Kingsway operated a course of its own for disaffected teenagers, but this was overtaken by administrative changes in April 1974. The course — another joint enterprise, involving the International Community Education Foundation and the ILEA — was, in fact, only one of the four lines of action that made up a special research project in community education. The basis of the project was to give educationally and socially disadvantaged school-leavers a boost in motivation via what the course team called 'environmental change'. A carefully-graduated build-up, with students attending college once a week for five weeks, led to a two week residential course. Students lived away from home in flats, organized their own cooking, and either went out to work or took part in work simulation exercises at the college. 'Whether the work is real or simulated,' said a course prospectus, 'the students will be expected to undertake a normal five-day working week for two weeks and to attend their work place for the normal working day of not less than six to eight hours per day.'

The Kingsway offering changed somewhat over the three years it was run. To begin with, it was specifically geared to truants — teenagers in their last year at school with a nonattendance rate of over 50 per cent. Later, some pupils who did attend school regularly were allowed in. Again, the first course the unit ran actually started off with the residential treatment, forty-two keen but homesick anti-schoolers in the depths of the countryside. 'It's still impressed on my brain,' said Mrs Merillie Huxley, the course director. 'The mistake we made was to force such a drastic environmental change. They were up all night because it was dark and they were frightened.'

Seen in action the course was blessedly unschool-like. A dozen boys and two impassive girls smoked, nattered sporadically at each other, and with reasonable grace allowed course tutor Miss Lorna Casey to explain what it was all about. She deftly fielded obscenities ('Don't worry, there's no ladies here — only girls'), and showed a videotaped film about a previous batch of students and the candle-making factory they set up. 'Hey, hey, there's David,' cried one of the viewers. 'He used to be at my school. Don't you remember — he played football and had whacking great feet.' Suspicion of Lorna and the whole enterprise took a body blow; a first, tenuous link between the course and the students' own world had been established.

Just as cooperation between all the agencies involved is the administrative key to London's struggle against truancy, so the establishment of trust between adult and truant is the educational key. Whatever guise curative informal education takes, its job is less than three-quarters done if such trust is lacking. In Mrs Huxley's words:

'The whole thing was a kind of descreening process, undoing all the things carrying over from school like calling people Sir, having to be there at nine in the morning. We were trying to create a more adult environment and a different kind of relationship with them, where they felt they were all equals and in it together.'

Mrs Fiona Green, another teacher who runs a special course for truants, puts it rather differently: one of her aims for her pupils is that they should 'be able to lose their mistrust of adults, which they had very strongly when I first met them'.

Mrs Green is the teacher in charge of the York Way Open Class, so called because it is exclusively for girl truants who live in York Way Court in North London. They should — but don't —,attend Starcross School. Attention was concentrated on York Way Court when it was discovered that the one block of flats housed no less than twelve nonattending pupils. The initial idea was arrived at jointly by the school, the education welfare service, and the local social services department, who were also worried about York Way. The Open Class's staff are a mixture of ILEA teachers and youth workers, and their aim is to 'reintroduce children to the simple discipline of getting to school and to find enjoyment and profit from and educational programme.' An Open Class day revolves round a system of meetings, to decide activities (a visit to the ILEA's television centre is planned, 'because Mary wants to be a film star'); to deal with problems, or to persuade the frequent gatecrashers that their presence is not

111

required. 'Usually one of the girls explains that the class is really just for York Way,' says Mrs Green, adding that, hopefully, it will sometime expand.

How is it working? At the time of writing, in early 1974, no Open Class student had actually volunteered to go back to Starcross. But after all the scheme had only been running for a term. On the other hand there were already signs that the relaxed atmosphere and lack of compulsion were having a desired effect. Attendance — apart from one terrible day just before Christmas, when the student roll dropped to three — is good. 'It's gone up to 80 per cent from nil,' says the acting head of Starcross, Miss Molly Barnett. More interesting still, some of the girls had started to say they wanted formal lessons. An English class was established forthwith. But the most important indication of all was an intangible, indefinable, nonstatistical one. The mistrust Mrs Green's pupils at first showed has now gone — 'We have a very good relationship.'

Any campaign against truancy must necessarily be of the hearts-and-minds order. As the ILEA point out, it's a slow job; and its true effects may not be known until the children of this generation's truants are old enough to show their own, parentally-determined, attitudes to formal education.

*Ruth Brandon*

# Local authority experiment: Liverpool

'Do you know what a social worker said to me the other day?' demanded an education welfare officer. 'He said, as long as the kids are all right and happy at home, then he's really not too worried about school. But my job *is* to be worried about school.'

I begin with this story because the social education team experiment in Liverpool has more to do with attitudes than anything else. And many of the attitudes it rejects are summed up in this story. The most important of these is the belief shared by many people (including teachers, pupils and this social worker at least) that school life and behaviour is quite separate from home life and behaviour.

This belief has many connections with truancy. At its simplest, when held by pupils, it will result in the kind of truancy described by Ian Berry, an educational psychologist:

'They feel that education hasn't much more to offer them. Perhaps they already have a part-time job and feel that to leave school would be better for them financially and in every other way. All you can do is to explain what will happen to a child and his parents if he doesn't go to school, and appeal to his sense of responsibility to go along with a situation that he basically disagrees with.'

The situation is worsened by the new school-leaving age. Schools which were already hard-pressed may not have introduced appropriate teaching programmes. Mrs Wilhelmina Willey, the chief education welfare officer for Liverpool's educational Area 4 says:

> 'There's a lot more truancy in the last year than there used to be. I think this is partly because the schools just don't have the right programmes to offer. And the kids are browned off because they're the first year that's had to stay on this long. I remember when they raised the leaving age to fifteen we had the same problem.'

This is perhaps the most common form of truancy. Education welfare officers may resent the time it takes up, and the perhaps pointless task of sending back to the classroom children who will shortly be leaving school for good. Most of the EWOs are more concerned with truants in the younger age groups, where the loss of education is a more serious matter, and where the underlying causes of truancy are almost certainly more complex.

In most of these cases, the social worker's attitude quoted at the beginning is nonsense: for if things are all right at home, then it is unlikely that they will be very far wrong at school. Mrs Willey estimates that 98 per cent of truancy can be related to home background stress rather than school.

A teacher, therefore, is likely to do both himself and the child a disservice if he adopts the home/school separation attitude and assumes that persistent absence on the part of one of his pupils is either his fault, the school's fault, or is simply due to the child's congenital laziness. And if the teacher believes that truancy is a problem which is generated within the school, and which can and should be contained and dealt with by the school, then his attitude to the education welfare officer dealing with the case may be less than helpful. He may dismiss the EWO as someone relatively unimportant whose job is simply to try and round up naughty children and bring them back into the fold where they will be dealt with. He may even resent the EWO as someone who is encroaching on his role.

The social worker, on the other hand, regards truancy as one of the least drastic manifestations of home stress. He may see the EWO as a bungling amateur, with no professional training, concerned with the narrowest of problems, who

114

possibly makes the social worker's jobs more difficult (for instance, by saturating the family with extra visits.)

As for the EWO, he finds himself in a most bewildering situation. He encounters mental or physical handicap, poverty, illness, delinquency, neglect — to name but a few of the main problems. But these are not situations with which he is qualified to deal. His instruments, persuasion, of parents and child, with the threat and possibly the actuality of prosecution to follow, tend to be rather blunt for the more delicate situations. He may, with experience, get to know the teachers and social workers concerned with some of the families with whom he has to deal, but he must do so on his own initiative for there is no framework within which such acquaintance and consultation is a matter of course. Prior to 1969 this was the situation in Liverpool as described by Derek Birley, then Deputy Director of Education:

'First, there were teachers in the schools, struggling to teach children but baulked by absences, misbehaviour, inability to respond and so on. There were education welfare officers who were called in to deal with cases of poor attendance, by referring back to a committee which considered whether to prosecute or not. There were doctors and nurses in the School Health Service concerned mainly with health problems but having all manner of information about children and their families as a result of their work, information that was either unused or used too late. There were psychologists and psychiatrists, social workers and remedial teachers, trying to diagnose and treat behaviour and learning problems. Their paths crossed those of children's officers, probation officers, the police juvenile-liaison officers and housing department officials, not to mention various voluntary agencies.

Each had a specialism and therefore a tendency to look at a child from that angle. Each worked within an administrative framework that encouraged him to reject cases falling outside his own ambit and to refer bigger problems back to his own headquarters rather than across to colleagues working in the field. At best, this seemed a recipe for inertia, for children falling between six or seven stools, perhaps being regarded as cases fitting (or not fitting) a particular professional and administrative outlook.'

While these circumstances were in no way peculiar to Liverpool, the city, under the guidance of Mr Birley, decided to do something about it and created the first social education team. The idea behind the team is to make better use of existing resources by clarifying roles, avoiding overlap between medical and welfare services, and removing procedural obstacles. The social education team concept is the logical consequence of recognizing that problems which manifest themselves in relation to education, as with truancy, may have roots and causes much wider and deeper than at first appear. What is needed is a framework for routine consultation between all relevant agencies. The social education team provides such a framework.

The only new post the team creates is that of education guidance officer. Les Davies is EGO for Area 4, the team of which Mrs Willey, Ian Berry, and the EWO quoted at the start are all members. He makes the point that it is almost impossible to define the job: each EGO, when appointed, had more or less to define it for himself, according to his own personality and the character of the area in which he worked:

'The EGO is the leader of the social education team. I'd loosely define myself as an educational trouble-shooter, that's to say, when a child's education is likely to be affected by anything at all, the school or the social services call me in. Various people see the symptoms of something going wrong, and my effort is to coordinate the efforts of all the agencies for the good of the child — and the school.'

Anyone who suspects something may be going wrong, but does not know quite whom to contact, may get in touch with Les Davies, who may not deal with the situation himself, but will bring it to the attention of someone who can and will. Thus it is hoped that cases of potential trouble may be caught in their early stages, before they have developed into something serious enough to demand the attention of, say, the Juvenile Courts, or to have involved the child's suspension from school.

The social education team recognizes that an apparently simple problem may have complex roots and is willing, indeed eager, to collect and collate any relevant information about a case from almost any source. But its prime concern is of course educational. The core of each team consists of the EWOs of that area; doctors, a senior nurse, an educational psychologist and psychiatric social workers attached to the child guidance and school psychiatric service; a remedial teaching team (whose role is very important indeed, since a child who stopped going to school for one reason may persist in staying away, even when the prime cause is cleared up, because he has fallen behind in his work and is afraid of looking foolish in front of his classmates); representatives of local social service departments; and the education guidance officer. These people all meet regularly to discuss their work, and to see which team members might best be brought in to deal with particular cases.

But if the team is to function competently it is essential that as many people as possible should know of its existence, be ready to trust it and cooperate with it — and this includes parents, social workers of all descriptions, and, above all, teachers.

The teachers play a crucial role in the successful functioning of the social education team. Derek Birley recognized this from the beginning:

'So far as teachers are concerned, the social education team seeks to involve them, not by appealing to their consciences and enlisting them as ancillary — and untrained — social workers, but by showing that involvement can help them to overcome children's learning problems. This might happen, for example, by using the services of a remedial teacher. This in itself might be helpful in showing a connection between a reading difficulty and an emotional problem. That advice, when linked with that of psychologist and social worker partners in the social education team, might open the doors to appreciation of complex and interrelated factors affecting a particular child and his family. In this setting, too, school attendance becomes something more than chasing up stragglers and prosecuting persistent offenders. An understanding of the reasons for absence may provide one of the earliest and best clues to a deep-seated and persistent problem that a number of agencies may separately have been facing. Again, at one level the social education team is a means of improving communication: at a deeper level it is something more valuable — a way of increasing understanding and sensitivity.'

In practice signs of trouble, such as withdrawal, misbehaviour, nonattendance or undue difficulty in learning, may indeed appear early on in the classroom. Faced with such signs, the teacher can be in something of a quandary. For one thing, sheer pressure of work may dictate his course of action — or the lack of it. Teachers, especially secondary school teachers in the kind of areas likely to produce most disturbed children, are often stretched to the limit. In this situation, they often feel there simply is not time to act as a sort of social worker as well. They may also feel that, given their limited time and the pressures upon them, the interests of the class as a whole must be paramount and on occasion override the interests of a particular pupil. This can lead to the kind of situation familiar to many EWOs, where some notably troublesome boy or girl is refusing to attend school, and much time and effort is being expended to get him or her back, in the full knowledge that the longer that child stays away, the happier the teacher will be, since this gives him at last an opportunity to get on with teaching the rest of the class.

The question of client confidentiality also comes up. Some social workers, for instance, may feel hesitant about co-operating with the team if they feel this means that the teacher will be given information about a child's family background which might endanger the social worker's own relationship with the family. This in the end boils down to a question of use and trust. Similarly, a headteacher may not feel that he should pass on information he has been given to the classteacher — though again, this is a problem more likely to crop up in junior schools, which are relatively small; in most secondary schools it is virtually impossible for the head not to delegate responsibility.

Some headteachers do feel somewhat defensive about the intervention of the EGO and his team. Les Davies admits,

'Occasionally we get the traditional headteacher, especially in junior schools, who likes to keep his problems to himself.' This may not necessarily be true of the classteacher, but she usually has to take her cue from the head, and so does the EWO, the member of the team most likely to be in regular contact with the school.

This, however, is an area where the activities of the EGO are making things easier for the rest of the team, especially the EWOs. The latter, especially in the more traditional schools, may find some difficulty about approaching the head on terms of professional equality, which is essential if any real contact is to be made. The education guidance officers, however, are all people who have had a great deal of professional teaching experience, and most of them have been headmasters (Les Davies was head of a comprehensive school before he took on this job).

Clearly, most of the cases dealt with by individual members of the team will not need to be brought to the attention of the team as a whole. Education welfare officers, remedial teachers and the rest will probably be able to deal with the greater proportion of the cases they come across much as they always have — though the knowledge that there are always other people available for consultation is a strength not to be underestimated. But the only member of the team constantly involved in team work is the EGO. As such, his view of the educational difficulties of his area is perhaps an odd one, since all the cases which come to his attention are complex, and many of them are urgent. The team's brief is to try to reach trouble at its source and take early concerted action, but that of course presupposes a halcyon situation where all current urgent priority cases have been dealt with, so that the team may concentrate on those which are not yet urgent, but which look as if they may become so.

Les Davies's time is devoted to the current top priority cases — he may be handling between forty and fifty at any one time. His day usually, begins with a consultation with his chief EWO Mrs Willey, and a large part of the rest of the day will be taken up by school visits, partly because headteachers are now finding out that they can approach him on all manner of problems, partly because the aim of the team is at all costs to avoid suspension which leaves such an indelible blot on a child's reputation.

119

So one typical day began with a visit to a junior school where one very disturbed child had been savagely attacking his peers and his teachers, who had reached the end of their tether:

'We brought in the psychologist, who diagnosed there was something wrong, but she wasn't sure what, and wasn't sure enough to call in the psychiatrist. Meanwhile, the headmistress wrote to the Education Department with a list of the kid's offences. I was called in as a sort of buffer, and went to see the parents and the school two or three times. The mother and the headmistress are no longer speaking. Meanwhile, we found out that the child couldn't read at all. So to give everyone time to think, we've tried to get him into an open-air special school. We've convinced the mother she should be considering the child's needs rather than her relationship with the school. Now the doctors must find something physically wrong with the child to get him in this school, which has small classes and so more attention, which is what the child is craving for. This removes the problem from the school, and helps mother not to have to leave work to look after the suspended child. So the way is smooth for thinking about the child's future needs.'

The rest of the morning was taken up by a visit to a secondary modern to arrange the transfer of two trouble-making boys to a nearby comprehensive. After the informal weekly team lunch Les Davies visited the home of a boy whose persistent nonattendance is going to get him suspended. His parents say they really don't mind if he goes to school or not, since if he doesn't he can always make himself useful to his Dad, who himself made it without benefit of schooling. At the end of three quarters of an hour's discussion, they seem to have been persuaded to send him to school. The rest of the day is spent at a comprehensive at the other end of the area, where Les Davies hopes to place a boy who has had an exceptionally difficult time with ill-health, truanted persistently, is now in a remand home, but seems about ripe to come out.

Do the social education teams work effectively? The answer would seem to be yes because the scheme was extended from the 1969 pilot largely because the attendance figures for the area improved considerably. But in many ways social education teams still have to establish themselves. For instance, one of the intentions was to avoid duplication of labour and visiting which would fit in with the new Seebohm recommendations about 'generic' rather than 'specialist' social work. But so far this has not entirely worked out in practice. For one thing, social workers are unlikely to leave a case entirely to an EWO, if only because the EWO's concerns are so relatively narrow (to which the EWO would reply that at least if you have a specific aim, you are likely to achieve it!). Mrs Willey sums up:

'Communication is better. Action is quicker. That's been happening for two years now. But there is still a certain amount of empire building partly encouraged by Seebohm and the introduction of the "generic" role. When there was the Children's Department and the Mental Health Department we could go to someone who we know had real expertise. Now everyone's supposed to know everything.'

The teams are very anxious that they should not be seen as 'yet another social service agency'. Their allegiance is very definitely to the education department — with all the advantages for the achievement of relatively narrow aims just discussed. But there seems little doubt that if a problem is viewed and approached in the round, rather than as a series of separated facets, the chances for solving it must be better, and the danger that a diagnosis will be made in complete ignorance of some important factor is reduced. And, of course, there is no reason why this should not be a two-way traffic. The education services benefit from the wider view of the other social services; they may also offer a way into some seemingly amorphous difficulty, by which a whole series of problems may be approached starting with the educational difficulties of particular children.

In the end, it boils down to a commonsense decision to consider the child as a whole and not as a possible manifestation of some particular handicap.

*Julia McGuinness*

# Out of school - what next?

The Education and Social Services Departments are cooperating in an exciting new venture — an experimental day centre for children between the ages of eleven and sixteen who are out of school. The centre will provide learning opportunities for a group of twelve to fifteen children based on their expressed needs. The centre will be community-orientated to break down the artificial barriers between learning and other activities of life. It will attempt to develop the child's self-confidence and ability to make decisions.

This extract is taken from an advertisement which appeared in December 1973 in a well-known London weekly publication. Such advertisements are becoming increasingly common. Phrases such as 'community-orientated' and 'artificial barriers' are becoming as ubiquitous as adventure playgrounds. From what source have these phrases and concepts sprung, and why is this trend towards new ventures increasing?

In the last few years one section of young people has become increasingly disillusioned with the current ethos of the education system and the adult values that shape the system. We are not dealing here with that small group of disturbed children whose problems lie in an area where psychotherapy is needed, but with that much larger group whose disillusionment is revealed by the increasing truancy figures. Why are these truants disillusioned, and why mainly at secondary school level?

Just as Christmas is an accepted recurring pattern in the mosiac of our culture, so at approximately five years of age every child is assumed to be prepared and willing to slot unquestioningly into an organization based, shaped and controlled by adult values. Research into children's growth has shown that children are attaining adolescence and puberty earlier; thus these children are biologically and socially ready to fulfil an adult role in society at an earlier age than, say, twenty years ago.

Present-day children with their fast maturing personalities and abilities to vocalize and feel strongly about their opinions find that many aspects of the education system are quite unrelated to their awareness and relationship with the adult environment at whose periphery they stand. Many resign themselves to this situation (though resignation is becoming more difficult now that the school leaving age has risen), but a growing number feel it worthwhile to opt out.

Repeating patterns emerge from discussion with various groups of truants. They will explain how artificial learning methods and formal teacher-pupil relationships are, for them, boring and a waste of time. They resent the mental and physical restrictions of the classroom situation; and they will describe tactics they employ to avoid discovery.

In the summer it is quite easy to meet truanting children; a stroll through local parks and commons reveals groups of youths idling away the time. They will often use their lunch money to pay for admission to the local swimming pool. When the weather is not so pleasant they gather in cafes, or wait until their homes are empty and spend the greater part of the day in the warmth. They play the waiting game for the postman, watching for the delivery of the morning mail, identifying the inevitable letter from the school, and destroying it before it gets into the hands of their parents. It is interesting to hear some truants talk of how they 'self-regulate' themselves, that is to say create a situation by which they benefit from the school situation to meet their expressed needs (as the advertisement calls the self-regulated demands of the children). They self-regulate themselves by attending morning and afternoon registration and lessons of interest and then absent themselves from those lessons of no appeal.

The education authorities, now finding themselves embarrassingly more and more unable to cope with the growing truancy trend by conventional means, have been looking for an alternative approach, one which does not create an even greater communication gap between the children and the school.

Searching for the roots of this alternative approach, names such as Homer Lane, Maria Montessori and particularly A. S. Neill come to mind. The education sections of public libraries comprehensively cover the work of these pioneers, so time will not be spent here describing their ideas and the schools they founded to put their ideas into practice. What will be examined is the present position and development of current alternative day schools and the people involved with them.

Many labels have been attached to the alternative schools, the most common being the 'free school'. Broadly speaking, the basic principles of the free school movement are as follows: the relationship between the adults and children in the free school is based on love and understanding, not on the use of artificial and unnecessary formalities; everyone is on first-name terms, and all members of the community regard themselves as equal members of the school.

It is widely accepted that for the preschool child, the fostering of the natural instincts of curiosity and learning leads to the most healthy and life-enhancing development. The free schools believe that exactly the same is true of the older\child; the physical and mental health and development of the child is best achieved in a stimulating environment in which self-regulation can operate. Therefore the atmosphere of the free school is such that the children have the opportunity to use the studies offered at the speed which suits them for as long as they are interested. Although it is the responsibility of the adults to provide a stimulating environment to foster the curiosity of the children, they are quite prepared for the children to suggest activities and projects either of the spur-of-the-moment type or of a more long-term nature.

The democratic heart of the school community lies in the school meeting, held weekly in most free schools. At this meeting matters arising out of the running of the school and the behaviour of the community are discussed and dealt with.

124

Matters that need a group decision are voted upon, with every member of the community, whether child or adult, having equal voting rights.

The actual involvement with the problems concerning the running of the school varies with the age of the children. For instance, the junior members of the community self-regulate their interests and involvement with school problems on an immediately comprehensible level, such as discussing and arranging school outings and the correct use of their library or quiet rooms, whereas older members of the community, with their broader understanding of the school's relationship with the community as a whole, will get themselves involved with such problems as how to deal with the bank overdraft (a problem unfortunately only too common in such schools), or the fact that there is not sufficient cash available to pay a much-needed extra staff member.

The actual borderline of involvement in relationship to age is not as absolute as in the above examples; for instance in one free school with which I was involved, all the children protested through the medium of the school meeting that they were not getting sufficient food for lunch. So, when the cook explained that the daily allocation of money for shopping appeared to be decreasing in its buying power, the community as a whole became involved with a financial matter. Thus it is through the school meeting that the children are able to share in the control and moulding of their surroundings.

Most free schools run as day schools encourage involvement of the parents; in fact some are parent-owned co-operatives. Not only does this mean that parents are welcome into the school at any time, it also facilitates the breakdown of more and more of the dividing lines and communication blocks between the school and home. Parental involvement may range from parents linking up their particular fields of knowledge with current interests of the children, or assisting staff with folk-singing or storytime etc, to extending the boundaries of the school's role in the community by using the school building to house additional requirements of the community, such as playgroups for preschool children etc.

The development of free schools in the last ten years falls into two distinct categories.

The first (usually those founded four or more years ago)

were established by groups of parents and teachers who wanted a self-regulating environment for their children, or in the case of the teachers, felt that their relationships with children and their teaching roles could be more healthily developed in a self-regulating atmosphere.

Although these schools are provisionally registered with the Department of Education and Science and have to meet the approval of a government inspector before they can be granted full registration, they receive no financial support from the state. Consequently their survival depends upon the parents raising enough money to purchase equipment and pay staff.

The second category of free schools is the type developed within last four years, where social workers and teachers are able to draw on some local authority facilities and obtain buildings and spaces usually at peppercorn rents. A small measure of support from local authorities has also been given in the way of equipment supplies and access to the school-meals service. These schools have no regular income, thus fund-raising schemes conducted by the parents and staff, and direct application to sympathetic groups are their main sources of cash.

Apart from attracting parents and children who wish to continue self-regulated development following the preschool years, free schools have been approached with growing frequency by parents of truanting children who, fearful of intervention by the authorities, and often themselves not in wholehearted sympathy with free school ideas, nevertheless hope that such schools may attract their children and have something to offer them. It is a well established syndrome that children transferring from an authoritarian situation to a self-regulating setting, find themselves disorientated for some weeks before they become aware of their own abilities to regulate themselves within the community; but once this period is over fairly healthy adjustment is achieved. Of course not every case of a truanting-child transfer is completely successful, but as most free school situations are without the structures that the child previously resented the overall impression is, after a settling-in period, that the child finds the school has something to offer him and, perhaps of even greater importance, he has something to offer the school.

Thus we have at the present time a situation of truanting

children at odds with a system that they identify as being intellectually and physically boring and irrelevant, a scattering of schools, that receive little or no aid from the authorities, struggling to offer an alternative and life-enhancing approach to education, and the various education and social services departments being forced to contemplate 'exciting new ventures' to deal with their growing problem.

Commenting on free schools recently, a member of the ILEA said:

'We feel at the present time we are unable to support them but I hope that we may nevertheless find a way to cooperate with them. I believe that we may have something to learn from their methods, of their skills in handling children and in forming relationships with children and of what can be added to our own schools.'

A tenuous recognition of free school methods is shown in the work of Alexander Bloom and those that followed him. At the end of the second world war Alexander Bloom was appointed headmaster of St George-in-the-East school in Stepney. In this area, which suffered much physical hardship during the war, he was given 260 children of both sexes from local primary schools. With a staff of ten teachers they worked to develop a community school; in fact the school developed into a community rather than a school. Much public criticism arose from his work but he was highly praised ·by A. S. Neill and others. The LCC considered his approach to be 'unorthodox', but gave him due recognition in that they sent him children who were considered to be 'difficult'. Sadly, after his death some ten years later there was no *direct* educational policy to continue the use of his work and ideas, or even to continue the school as it had developed under his guidance.

Countesthorpe College in Leicestershire, a mixed school taking children from eleven, has incorporated many ideas of the free school movement. The involvement of the pupils through the school meeting is developing through their meeting system called the 'moot'. At present only the staff have voting rights at the moot, though students attend and speak. Ways and means of extending student participation are under review. At present students' voting powers are restricted to the school council, where the elected student majority vote on nonacademic affairs. The ethos of the school puts great stress on the children developing a sense of awareness and self-discipline in relation to the school community and the community at large.

In the London area one school has taken the open-plan arrangement to develop the ethos of activity and self-regulation to replace the pattern of knowledge to be acquired and facts to be stored. On visiting the school, one is conscious of the relaxed relationship between staff and pupils (all on first-name terms) based on friendship and mutual sharing of experiences, and although the school is not completely self-regulating one feels very strongly the background from which they have developed their 'unorthodox' ideas. Many of the barriers between home and school have been broken down: parents are welcome at any time during the school day and the school buildings are in constant use in the evenings when parents and staff meet and use the facilities. Once again this approach is earning recognition as a centre for aid and refuge for truanting children who are transferred there from other schools.

Past discussions as to whether free school ideas could be carried over to the state system have often lacked impact because it has been argued that theory could not be put into practice, and also because on the whole children have appeared to be satisfied with the present system. Now that statistics clearly indicate an increasing number of children are not happy with the present system, and now that it has been clearly shown that free school ideas can thrive within the state system, would it not produce a more healthy educational dialogue to give official recognition and support to free schools and those who work in them?

Yet financially, ILEA teachers who are seconded to the various schemes for helping truanting children receive grant aid from the ILEA on condition that the schemes (based on self-regulating principles) aim to get the children back into the schools they have rejected. It would be more reasonable and socially productive to insist that 'alternative unorthodox' ideas on education be officially accepted and available to *all* in *all* schools so that the roots of truancy can be eliminated.

128